simply
beautiful

WITHDRAWN

weddings

50 PROJECTS TO
PERSONALIZE YOUR WEDDING

heidi boyd

NORTH LIGHT BOOKS
CINCINNATI, OHIO
www.artistsnetwork.com

10 09 08 07 06   5 4 3 2 1

Distributed in Canada by Fraser Direct
100 Armstrong Avenue
Georgetown, ON, Canada L7G 5S4
Tel: (905) 977-4411

Distributed in the U.K. and Europe by David &
Charles
Brunel House, Newton Abbot, Devon, TQ12 4PU,
England
Tel: (+44) 1626 323200, Fax: (+44) 1626 323319
Email: postmaster@davidandcharles.co.uk

Distributed in Australia by Capricorn Link
P.O. Box 704, S. Windsor, NSW 2756 Australia
Tel: (02) 4577-3555

        Library of Congress Cataloging-in-Publication
Data

Boyd, Heidi
   Simply beautiful weddings / Heidi Boyd.
        p. cm.
   Includes index.
   ISBN-13: 978-1-58180-771-4
   ISBN-10: 1-58180-771-6
   1. Handicraft. 2. Wedding decorations. I. Title.
   TT149.B69 2006
   745.594'1--dc22
                            2006009748

Editor: Jessica Gordon
Layout Artist: Jessica Schultz
Production Coordinator: Greg Nock
Photographers: Christine Polomsky and Tim Grondin
Photo Stylist: Nora Martini

metric conversion chart

TO CONVERT	TO	MULTIPLY BY
Inches	Centimeters	2.54
Centimeters	Inches	0.4
Feet	Centimeters	30.5
Centimeters	Feet	0.03
Yards	Meters	0.9
Meters	Yards	1.1
Sq. Inches	Sq. Centimeters	6.45
Sq. Centimeters	Sq. Inches	0.16
Sq. Feet	Sq. Meters	0.09
Sq. Meters	Sq. Feet	10.8
Sq. Yards	Sq. Meters	0.8
Sq. Meters	Sq. Yards	1.2
Pounds	Kilograms	0.45
Kilograms	Pounds	2.2
Ounces	Grams	28.4
Grams	Ounces	0.04

F+W PUBLICATIONS, INC.

ABOUT THE
author

Heidi Boyd is an experienced designer who specializes in creating accessible and elegant projects ideal for the beginning crafter or for anyone who is pressed for time. Her projects have been featured in many of the **BETTER HOMES AND GARDENS** publications, and Heidi has also appeared on **HOME & GARDEN TELEVISION** demonstrating projects from her books.

Look for her other titles in the Simply Beautiful series, **SIMPLY BEAUTIFUL GREETING CARDS**, **SIMPLY BEAUTIFUL RIBBON-CRAFT**, **SIMPLY BEAUTIFUL BEADED JEWELRY** and, of course, the wildly successful **SIMPLY BEAUTIFUL BEADING**, a Booklist top ten craft book for 2004. Heidi's other titles include her family-friendly books **WIZARD CRAFTS**, **FAIRY CRAFTS** and **PET CRAFTS**.

After years of working as a project designer and teaching art classes in the Midwest, Heidi now enjoys life near the Maine coast with her husband, their three children and the family dog.

DEDICATED TO...

my darling Jon, without whom I'd never have come to understand what true love and marriage are all about. I hope each of our three children finds the love of someone special who treasures them as we treasure them and each other.

acknowledgments · Photographing this book while eight months pregnant in an August heat wave could have been disastrous if not for the good-humored understanding of Jessica Gordon and Christine Polomsky. Not only are they experts in their fields, but they also recognized the importance of restorative ice cream breaks. I owe thanks to Donna Dennison and Yvonne Naanep for sharing their brilliant ideas that added projects to the pages. As always, I also credit the photo stylist, Nora Martini, and the page layout artist, Jessica Schultz, who make my work look so good!

contents

Joanna Dower
&
Matthew Masterson

together with our parents
William and Jacquelyn Dower & Vincent and Pamela Masterson
request the pleasure of your company as we celebrate our marriage on
Saturday, July 30, two thousand and five at
five-thirty in the afternoon

Omni Hotel
676 N. Michigan Avenue
Chicago, Illinois
ation to follow

introduction

It seems unreal that fifteen years have passed since the day I married Jon—I can still clearly recall the details of the ceremony and reception. Since our wedding, our love has grown in ways I couldn't have imagined, and together we've created a large, happy family. As joyful as the occasion is, it can also be stressful, so it's no wonder that many brides become anxious at the daunting task of planning their nuptials. The key to keeping everything in perspective is to simply remember that if your heart is filled with love, the rest is just details.

Take a deep breath and enjoy the planning process! Whether the setting is casual or elegant, in this book you'll find decorations, favors, keepsakes, wearable accessories and jewelry to bring unique, creative touches to your celebration. Every project is simple enough for the complete novice. If you've never worked with ribbon, silk flowers, beads or scrapbook papers, this is the perfect time to start. You might even come away with a new crafting pursuit.

Handcrafted projects add charm and originality to your wedding and also save you money. I keenly remember the endless wait for our wedding day. In hindsight, I should have endeavored to create more wedding projects—it might've helped those long days before the ceremony to pass more quickly.

Here's a heartfelt wish for wedding crafting success, but even more importantly, for many happy years of wedded bliss.

basic supplies

All the projects in this book can be divided into three general categories: papercrafting, silk flower arranging and jewelry making. Some of the supplies can be used for multiple kinds of crafts, and some are more specialized. Listed on the following pages, you'll find descriptions and images of the most common supplies used for the crafting projects in this book.

papercrafting supplies

You need just a few supplies to get started in papercrafting. If you're a scrapbooker or a cardmaking enthusiast, you probably already have the basic materials on hand.

embellishments

|CARDSTOCK| This heavyweight paper is easily scored with a stylus. Its inherent strength makes it ideal for cards and favor boxes.

|PRINTED SCRAPBOOK PAPER| Visit scrapbooking and craft stores to appreciate the range of printed papers available in either 8" × 10" (20cm × 25cm) or 12" × 12" (30cm × 30cm) size. Whatever your color scheme and budget, you're sure to find embossed and glittered pages to fit your wedding.

|VELLUM| Featherweight translucent vellum sheets instantly add dimension to cards and papercrafts. Manufactured in a variety of colors and designs, vellum sheets are also commonly embossed with patterns or embellished with sparkling glitter. Use adhesives intended for vellum paper—traditional glues and tapes may be visible through the translucent sheet.

|DOUBLE-SIDED TAPE| For assembling cards, I've found double-stick tape less messy than glue.

|SCISSORS| The key to papercrafting success is a pair of sharp scissors. It's handy to have several pairs in a range of sizes. A small pair that fits comfortably in your hand and has sharp points suited for cutting out intricate patterns is ideal.

|INKPADS AND STAMPS| Spare yourself the struggle of creating perfect handwriting on your cards by keeping a selection of message stamps and a simple black inkpad at the ready for adding an instant greeting. As hand stamping can sometimes go wrong, it's a good idea to stamp your card first—that way if you slip up, no work is wasted.

|EMBELLISHMENTS| The popularity of scrapbooking and card-making has increased the availability of wedding-themed charms, printed messages and paper cutouts available in stores. These ready-made decorations add instant elegance to your projects. Just be sure they're firmly anchored with an appropriate glue.

|PAPER TRIMMERS| I use a 12" (30cm) craft paper trimmer. The ruled grid lines on the paper trimmer make cutting cards, rectangles and squares a breeze.

|CRAFT KNIFE| A few projects call for the use of a craft knife, a pencil-like tool with a sharp, angled blade. A sharp blade is essential, requiring less pressure and making cutting safer.

|STYLUS| A handy little tool with a metal ball on the end, a stylus is used to create an instant fold line. Just press it into the paper along the line where you want the paper to fold.

papers from left to right: printed scrapbook paper, vellum, heavyweight gold paper, vellum

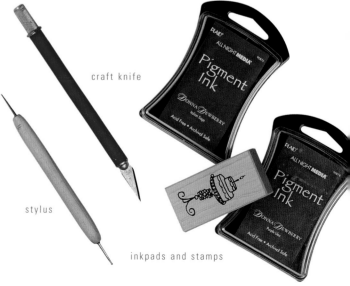

craft knife

stylus

inkpads and stamps

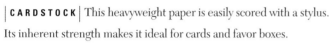

supplies for working with silk flowers

Crafting with silk flowers is surprisingly easy. You need a minimal amount of supplies to create beautiful arrangements and bridal accessories.

|SILK FLOWERS| No matter your color scheme, you're sure to find coordinating silk flowers. Not all silk flowers are constructed the same way—consider using varieties with paperlike petals or wire-cored petals that can be individually positioned.

|FLORAL TAPE| This strong clothlike tape comes in either white or green. It doesn't feel sticky to the touch, but with tight wrapping the tape firmly bonds to itself.

|FLORAL FOAM BRICKS| In this book, I use dry floral foam to anchor silk flower stems in position. Use a serrated knife to cut floral foam into the proper size.

|CORSAGE PINS| These simple straight pins with pretty pearl-like tops are used to secure silk flower stems together, or to secure ribbon around the stems of a bouquet.

|FLORAL WIRE| Available in either green or white, this bend- able, fabric-wrapped wire is deceptively soft to the touch. The wire core has the strength to coil, wrap and connect silk floral stems together. Be sure to select the appropriate gauge wire for the task. For example, lightweight floral wire is used in the bridal shower invitations.

|WIRE CUTTERS| Save your scissors blades and use sturdy wire cutters to easily cut through floral wire and silk flower stems. You may be able to use your jewelry wire cutters for small silk flower stems, but you'll need a larger cutter to trim other varieties of silk flowers that have thick wire embedded in their stems.

floral tape

corsage pins

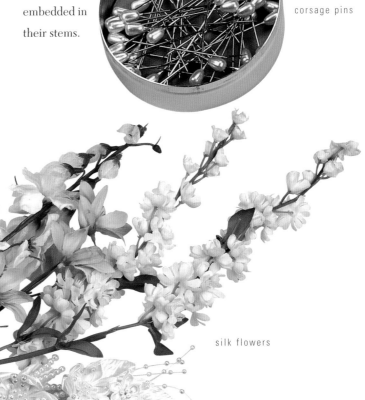

floral foam brick

silk flowers

jewelry-making supplies

If you're not already a beader, your upcoming wedding might be the perfect inspiration to get you started. Each project will require its own beads, but they all share the same few basic tools.

"E" beads

glass pearls

beads

It's easy to be overwhelmed by the huge selection of beads in craft stores. The following descriptions should help guide you in purchasing the specific bead varieties used in this book.

|FRESHWATER PEARLS| Natural freshwater pearls come in many irregular shapes and sizes. Although white is the most common color, they're also available in gray, pink and violet. Purchase them by the strand or individually.

|GLASS PEARLS| Uniformly round, glass pearls make an inexpensive substitute to real cultured pearls.

|GLASS SEED BEADS| These very small, inexpensive beads come in a wide range of colors and finishes. Seed beads are most commonly sold in plastic tubes.

|JAPANESE SEED BEADS| Larger than standard seed beads and smaller than "E" beads, Japanese seed beads come in beautiful colors and finishes. They're most commonly found in bead stores. If you can't find them, substitute smaller "E" beads.

|"E" BEADS| Like seed beads, inexpensive "E" beads are available in a wide range of colors and finishes. Larger in size than seed beads, they are quicker to string.

|CRYSTALS| Faceted crystal beads reflect light and add sparkle to any beaded piece. They come in round, cube and bicone shapes. The prices of these beads vary dramatically: The more expensive varieties, such as Swarovski, are clearer and more reflective than generic crystal beads.

|GLASS BEADS| In addition to the largely white glass beads used in the bridal jewelry pieces in this book, glass beads come in an enormous range of styles, colors, finishes and sizes. Some glass beads are pressed, and others have a multicolored finish. Often it's more economical to buy mixed packages instead of individual beads.

findings

Jewelry findings are an integral part of beading. Take advantage of ornate findings set with rhinestones and pearls to complement formal bridal jewelry.

|HEAD PINS AND EYE PINS| Head pins have a flat end and eye pins have a looped end. Used to make dangles and to link beads, both are sold in different lengths in gold and silver finishes. Sterling varieties are easiest to shape.

|CLASPS| A myriad of different clasps is available. Be sure to select one that matches the scale and style of your beadwork. A few varieties of clasps include multistrand clasps, toggle and "O" ring clasps and filigree clasps.

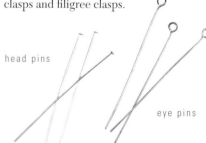

head pins

eye pins

stone chips

crystals

lobster clasps

toggle clasp

larger gold and silver crimp tubes

| CRIMP BEADS AND CRIMP TUBES |
Round crimp beads or cylindrical crimp tubes are strung onto either end of a strand to attach the clasp. Select a crimp tube wide enough to accommodate two widths of the stringing wire.

| EARRING FINDINGS | Available in both gold and silver finishes, there are findings for both pierced and unpierced ears. Some varieties of earring findings include post earrings, French earwires and lever-back earrings.

stringing materials

Stringing materials are crucial to the strength and appearance of finished pieces. Follow the listed materials for each project for the best results. You can always change the color, but stick with the specified product type to ensure success.

| BEADALON STRINGING WIRE | This strong wire has a steel core coated with smooth, flexible nylon, and it comes in a variety of sizes. Thinner wire is ideal for stringing smaller beads, and thicker wire is best for heavier beads.

| SILK CORD | Look for silk cord pre-strung with a flexible beading needle. Choose cord that passes easily through your selected beads.

| 26-GAUGE WIRE | Narrow enough to easily pass through even the smallest beads, yet strong enough to twist and hold them in place, this flexible sterling wire is perfect for beadwork.

tools

Of the many specialty tools on the market, only a few are really necessary to get started with beadwork. I strongly suggest purchasing round-nose pliers, chain-nose pliers and wire cutters. You should be able to make almost all the projects in the book using just these three tools.

| ROUND-NOSE PLIERS | With their two smooth, round, tapered pincers, round-nose pliers facilitate shaping wire into coils, circles or loops.

| CHAIN-NOSE PLIERS | The pointed pincers of chain-nose pliers are commonly used in wire jewelry projects. They're perfect for holding jewelry while wire ends get wrapped. In all the necklace and bracelet projects in this book, chain-nose pliers are used to squeeze crimp tubes flat.

| WIRE CUTTERS | Specially made for jewelry work, wire cutters are used to trim wires and link chains. It's safer to make a quick clip with wire cutters than to exert too much pressure with scissors blades.

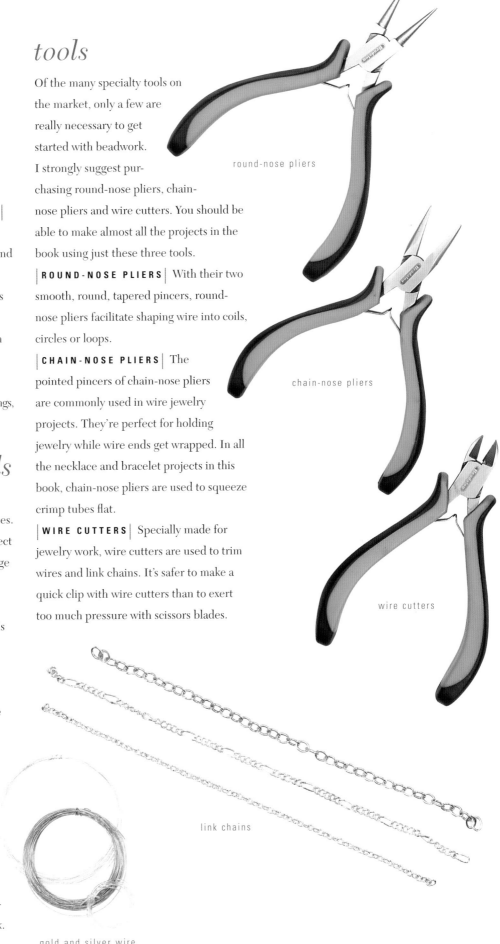

round-nose pliers

chain-nose pliers

wire cutters

link chains

gold and silver wire

basic techniques

Once you've amassed the necessary tools and supplies, you're ready to learn some basic techniques. Look over the simple techniques for each crafting category so you'll be ready to tackle projects in any chapter. If it's your first time using the tools, practice with scraps before using special papers, ribbon or jewelry findings.

papercrafting techniques

You've held and written on paper your entire life, but if this is your first time converting it into cards and boxes, you'll need to become familiar with a paper trimmer, stylus and ruler to achieve professional-looking results.

SCORING AND FOLDING PAPER

one · Copy the template at the correct enlargement and cut it out. Trace around the template onto the back of the paper that you are using to make your project, including all fold lines. Cut out the shape with sharp scissors.

two · Line a straightedge up with the fold lines you drew on the back of your paper. Drag the ball end of a stylus along the straightedge to create a score line.

three · Fold along the score lines to create the object you are making.

techniques for working with silk flowers

Many of the projects in the Accessories chapter require you to pull apart silk flowers. It does seem counterintuitive to decimate an attractive flower, but by removing the plastic stem and flower center, you won't diminish the flower's attractiveness. Loose petals can easily be sewn or glued to almost any surface, and the new flowers will feature beautiful bead or rhinestone centers.

SEPARATING SILK FLOWER COMPONENTS

one · Position a pair of wire cutters just below the flower head, and snip the flower off the stem. If you're making the card cake (page 48) or the rose barrette (page 80), stop here and glue the intact flower heads in place.

two · Pull the green plastic leaf cap off the underside of the flower. Carefully slide each petal off the plastic flower center.

three · Clear plastic cups are often interspersed between the petals to give a silk flower dimension. When taking the flower apart, just slide them out of the way, and continue gently removing the remaining petals. Once you've finished, discard all the plastic pieces, along with the green leaves. Try to avoid mixing up your flowers by restacking each set of petals from largest to smallest before continuing on to the next flower head.

jewelry-making techniques

Jewelry making is deceptively easy, so try not to be intimidated by your new tools. With a little practice, you'll be wielding your tools like a professional. Learn the following simple techniques, and you'll be well on your way to making fabulous jewelry.

using crimp tubes

Stringing wire and metal crimps ensure that your beaded creations are secure. It's almost impossible to break wire core strands, and crimps eliminate the need for knots. Once pressure is applied to a crimp, the flattened metal tightly traps the strand ends in place.

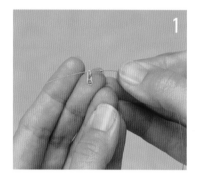

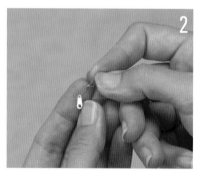

one · String one crimp bead or tube followed by one part of the clasp onto the end of the strand. Position them about ½"–1" (1cm–3cm) from the end of the wire.

two · Fold the strand end back through the crimp bead or tube. Pull the end to tighten the loop with the clasp.

three · Separate the wires inside the crimp bead or tube so they rest against opposite sides of the crimp (wires should not cross inside the crimp). Clamp the crimping pliers (or just use chain-nose pliers) over the outside of the bead or tube. Squeeze the crimping tool or chain-nose pliers to flatten the bead or tube to trap the wire securely. Carefully cut off the remaining wire end flush with the edge of the crimp tube.

turning a head pin loop

This is the easiest way to shape the end of a beaded head pin. With a simple turn of the wrist, the wire end is wrapped around the end of your round-nose pliers to create a small, even loop.

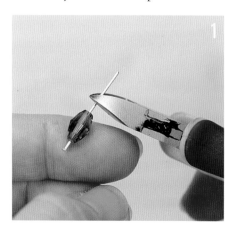

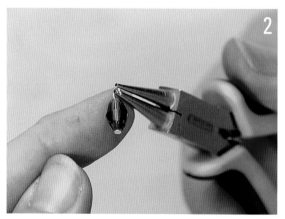

one · Slide a bead onto a head pin. Use wire cutters to cut the head pin wire to about ⅜" (1cm) above the bead. (For larger beads, cut the wire to about ¼" [6mm].)

two · Grab the head pin wire near the end with round-nose pliers and twist them toward yourself to create a loop. Use round-nose and chain-nose pliers to make fine adjustments to secure the loop.

making a wrapped loop

The extra step necessary to make a secure wrapped loop is often worth the effort. Just turning a loop will allow you to quickly hook beads onto an earring finding, but with wear the loop can open. A wrapped loop is tightly wired shut and will not open with wear.

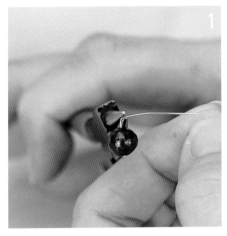 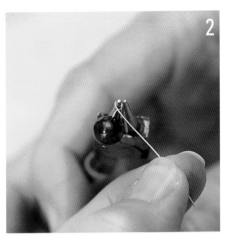 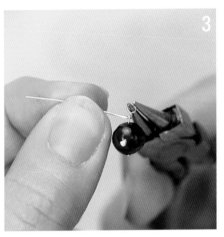

one · Slide a bead onto a head pin and bend the wire above the bead at a 90° angle with round-nose pliers.

two · Wrap the wire around the nose of the round-nose pliers to create a loop.

three · Hold the loop with the round-nose pliers and use your fingers or chain-nose pliers to wrap the tail end of the wire around the base of the loop. Trim away excess wire with wire cutters.

opening and closing jump rings

Jump rings are very handy connectors that give your jewelry a professional finish. They can pull open with pressure, so it's important not to weaken the metal by hooking them together improperly. If you follow the steps below, you'll avoid this common mistake.

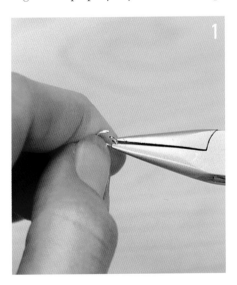 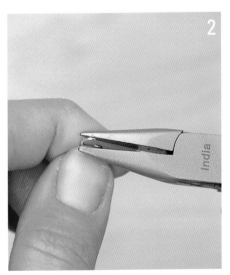

one · Hold one side of the jump ring between your thumb and index finger, just below the break in the metal. Grab the other side of the jump ring with your fingers or with chain-nose pliers, and pull the wire toward you to open it. Be careful not to open the jump ring by pulling the wire ends away from each other, as horizontal action can distort the shape of the jump ring and weaken it.

two · Close the jump ring by sandwiching the wires between the pincers of the chain-nose pliers. Apply even pressure to bring the wire ends firmly back together.

decorations & favors

I t's easy to be overwhelmed by the prospect of decorating for your reception, so cut the job in half by creating table toppers that double as favors. Baked or purchased goodies elegantly packaged in handmade paper containers make perfect decorations and are sure guest-pleasers. Choose from paper cones, pillow boxes, pyramids or purse-shaped boxes to arrange into a large centerpiece grouping or to decorate individual place settings.

I've always loved fresh flowers, but I have to admit that silk versions have become very attractive. One of the greatest advantages of using silk flowers is that all your arrangements can be made ahead of time, sparing you the anxiety of last-minute preparations. Any of the arrangements in this chapter can easily be converted for fresh flowers—simply substitute oasis for floral foam and insert a waterproof liner inside the container.

With both floral decorations and favors, think of ways to tailor your choices to your celebration. For instance, find a local candy maker who makes shell-shaped confections to package inside your favor boxes for an oceanside wedding. If you're having a fall wedding, bend natural bittersweet branches into heart wreaths to decorate the church, or make Christmas ornament place cards for a holiday reception. Whatever the season or locale, capitalize on what's readily available.

CHAPTER

willow heart wreath

MATERIALS

four approx. 20" (51cm) sections of white berry garland (each garland makes three to four wreaths)

½" (1cm) wide off-white wired grosgrain ribbon

16" (41cm) of ¼" (6mm) wide green silk ribbon

silk rose leaves (salvaged from discarded silk flower stems)

hot glue gun and melt sticks

*tip > Look for budding branches that fit your wedding color scheme. For example, orange and red bittersweet branches are widely available in the fall, and holly-berry boughs are commonplace at Christmas. During the holidays, also be on the lookout for plain red berry branches to make valentine wreaths. You'll find that pastel-colored ber-ries are popular in the springtime. Off-white bows and green hanging ribbons complement any of these color options.

Add a touch of romance to your ceremony with these budding wreaths. Hang them in doorways, on chair backs or over windowpanes. Be sure to save a few wreaths, and present them to friends and family who will enjoy hanging them in their homes as a memento of your wedding.

one • Cut four branches of white berry sprigs to approximately 16" to 18" (41cm to 46cm) each. Place two branches on each side of your work surface and twist the bottoms of all four branches together to make the pointed bottom of the heart.

two • Cut a 2½' (76cm) length of cream ribbon. Curve the free ends of the branches in toward each other to form a heart shape, and secure the ends with the ribbon. Tie the ribbon in a bow to secure the heart shape.

three • Twist each green tendril around a pencil to create decorative curlicues. Arrange the tendrils to frame the heart shape.

four • Pull several leaves from some silk flowers and hot glue them to the brown stems around the wreath.

five • Turn the wreath over so the back side is facing up. Tie one end of the ¼" (6mm) wide green ribbon around several branches and knot it. Repeat for the other end of the ribbon to finish the hanger.

lovebird centerpiece

MATERIALS

small table trunk

one silk flowering dogwood stem cut into five individual stems

green reindeer moss

1¾" (4cm) bird's nest

two small white doves

2¾" x 3⅞" x 3⅞" (7cm x 10cm x 10cm) floral foam brick (FloraCraft)

hot glue gun and melt sticks

serrated-edge knife

wire cutters

❋ *tip* > Regardless of the flower selection, surprise your guests by adding a couple of whimsical silk butterflies or birds amongst the petals. Look for inventive containers for your arrangements, such as teacups, that can be reused and enjoyed for years to come.

At first glance, this elegant, Asian-inspired centerpiece simply appears to be artistically arranged flowers. However, once seated, guests will be enchanted to discover a small bird's nest with a miniature pair of doves nestled in the flowering branches. Silk flowers ensure that the centerpieces can easily be made ahead of time.

one · Use a serrated-edge knife to cut the foam to a size that fits into the chest. Slide the cut foam into the open trunk.

two · Cut the dogwood stem into five different-sized flowering branches. Discard the heavyweight center stem.

three · Arrange the stems in a pleasing arrangement by anchoring them in the floral foam brick. Place a taller stem to one side of the back to give the arrangement height, and let some flowers and buds drape over the sides of the trunk.

four · Hot glue green reindeer moss over the exposed foam to cover it.

five · Hot glue the nest into the branches and then hot glue the doves into the nest.

flapper purse centerpiece

MATERIALS

beaded purse 6" (15cm) high, 5" (13cm) wide, 2¾" (7cm) deep

silk flower stems: three rose delphinium, five off-white cosmos, two brown roses

greenery, including leaves and small buds

floral foam brick (FloraCraft)

serrated knife

hot glue gun and melt sticks

wire cutters

tip > Beaded purses are available in a host of colors and styles, making it easy to find a variety of designs that coordinate with your color scheme. Don't overlook import and thrift stores for less expensive alternatives.

Perfect for an elegant evening wedding, these unique centerpieces are sure to garner compliments from every female guest. Under the silk flowers, the beaded purse sparkles and reflects the tabletop candlelight. The silk flower stems are simply anchored in a foam block tucked inside the purse. Once the arrangement is removed, the purse is just like new, and will beautifully accessorize your formal wardrobe on special occasions.

one · Use a serrated knife to cut a piece of green floral foam to fit inside the purse you've chosen. (Use a purse that has a wide bottom and can stand up on its own.)

two · Fit the foam snugly into the purse. Cut off a little more foam if necessary to make the block fit.

three · Cut all the flowers off the heavyweight center stems. Place three red, long-stemmed delphinium into the floral foam, keeping them in a central position.

four · Place the brown roses around the red flowers.

five · Place the off-white cosmos into the arrangement. Rotate the purse to ensure that the flowers are evenly distributed.

six · Fill in the bouquet with green leaves and small buds. Fill in the edges of the bouquet with green leaves. If the leaf stems aren't securely anchored into the foam, hot glue them in place.

seashell centerpiece

MATERIALS

3¾" (10cm) wide x 5¾" (15cm) high rectangular glass vase

blue-purple silk hydrangea stems

bleached beaded sea grass

assorted shells

12 fl. oz. clear floral-arranging compound (Everlasting Elegance)

wire cutters

tip > To adapt this project to fit your unique wedding location, consider placing smooth pebbles from a river or lakefront location into clear vases, and top the arrangement with green foliage.

P erfect for an oceanside celebration, these center-pieces bring the beauty of the coastline to reception tables. Place collected shells in a clear glass vase and fill it with everlasting water to accentuate the natural colors. The vase is topped with a sea of blue hydrangea flowers and punctuated with sparkling beaded seagrass.

one · Place an assortment of shells in the bottom of a glass vase. Fill the vase about one third full with shells arranged haphazardly. Make sure to place the shells that you want to be most visible along the edges of the vase.

two · Carefully read the floral-arranging compound instructions, and mix it together in a large disposable bowl. Pour the gel-like compound into the vase. Leave the top halves of some of the shells uncovered by the gel.

three · Use the wire cutters to trim the hydrangea so that the flowers rest at the top of the vase, and discard any leaves. Place the hydrangea flowers into the vase, securing the stems in the shell base.

four · Cut the sea grass to a height that works for the arrangement, and thread each individual stem down into the shell base. Allow the compound to set overnight, or as per the instructions on the package.

beaded candle rings

MATERIALS

about 24" (61cm) 26-gauge silver wire

pink semiprecious bead chips

green Japanese seed beads

wire cutters

tip > Stone chips are very irregular in size. Be flexible in how many you use to make each flower.

Large stone chip beads quickly loop together to make uniquely shaped flowers in these delicate candle rings. Blooming from a glistening stem of green seed beads, each translucent flower captures and reflects candle-light across the tabletop. You may customize the length of your beaded strands to fit precisely around the votives you choose, or you may prefer the appearance of wrapping them several times around the candle base.

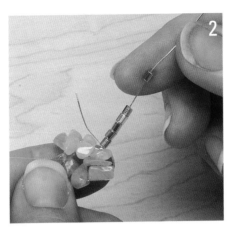

one • Thread nine to ten pink stone chip beads onto the 24" (61cm) length of 26-gauge silver wire. Twist the short end of wire around the long end to make and secure the first bead flower.

two • Thread on five to six green Japanese seed beads to make a short stem.

three • Thread on 13 green Japanese seed beads and then twist the wire around the base of the stem to form a loop-shaped leaf.

four • Thread on five to six more green Japanese seed beads to make another stem. Thread on more stone chips to make another flower, and continue in the pattern as established.

five • Continue beading until the candle ring is long enough to wrap around a votive candleholder, ending with a leaf. Trim the wire end and make sure it is twisted securely around the base of the leaf, as this twist will secure the entire design. To secure the beaded strand around the candle, twist the ends loosely together.

ANOTHER SIMPLY BEAUTIFUL IDEA

Use mother-of-pearl chip beads to make a more muted version of this candle ring. The finished flexible vine of wired flowers and leaves can be quickly wrapped around cake server handles or toasting glass stems to transform plain pieces into custom wedding accessories.

romantic paper cones

MATERIALS

patterned scrapbook paper
(Anna Griffin)

sturdy cardstock

pink wild rose silk flower stem

10" (25cm) of $\frac{1}{8}$" (3mm)
wide green satin ribbon

Aleene's Tacky Glue

hot glue gun and melt sticks

stylus, bone folder or embossing tool

$\frac{1}{8}$" (3mm) paper punch

wire cutters

straightedge

scissors

pencil

Surprise your guests with these traditional Victorian paper cones. Historically presented to loved ones at holidays, they're perfectly suited for weddings. Purchase an attractive assortment of candies to pour into each folded paper cone. Arrange the finished cones in a circle like wedges of a cake, or hang them individually off a raised-post chair back.

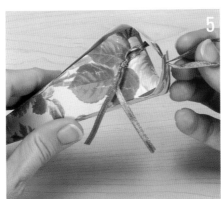

ANOTHER SIMPLY BEAUTIFUL IDEA

Take advantage of the wide assortment of scrapbook papers, and select the perfect paper color and design for your wedding. This demure pale paper cone topped with an off-white rose makes the perfect decorative favor for a traditional reception.

one · Copy the pattern on page 125 onto a piece of sturdy cardstock at the proper size. Cut out the pattern to make a template. Trace the pattern onto the back of the scrapbook paper you choose. Trace the fold lines onto the paper as well. Cut out the cone.

two · Use a stylus or a bone folder and a straightedge to score the paper along the fold lines.

three · Fold the paper into the cone shape along the fold lines. Glue the narrow flap under the open edge of the cone.

four · Fold up the flaps at the top of the cone and punch a hole in the middle where the flaps intersect.

five · Fold the 10" (25cm) length of ribbon in half, and tie the ends in an overhand knot. Thread the loop end up through the holes you punched in the top of the cone. The knot will prevent the hanging loop from pulling out through the holes.

six · Cut a pink silk rose from its stem with wire cutters, and hot glue it to the top of the paper cone.

puffy favor boxes

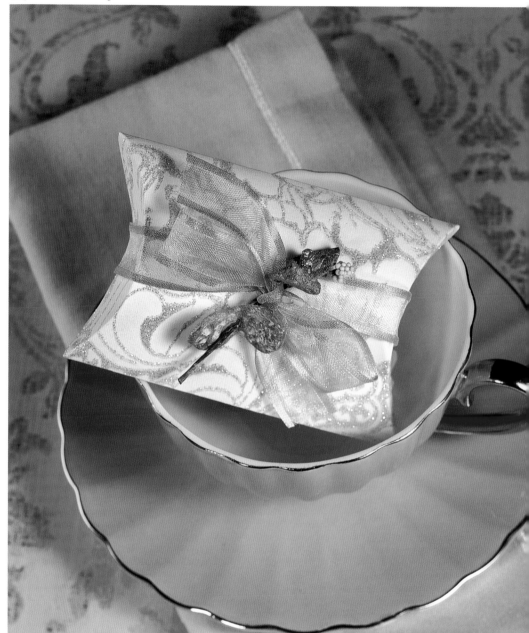

MATERIALS

cardstock scrapbook paper (Florence flat glitter paper, K&Company)

sturdy cardstock

silk eucalyptus branch (Darice)

½" (1cm) wide gold-edged organdy ribbon

Aleene's Tacky Glue

stylus, bone folder or embossing tool

wire cutters

scissors

pencil

ANOTHER SIMPLY BEAUTIFUL IDEA

You can always find scrapbook paper to coordinate with your wedding color scheme. In this variation, I used a heavyweight gilded green cardstock to make a sturdy box. These small-sized boxes let you take advantage of widely available inexpensive spools of ⅛" (3mm) narrow ribbon.

Good things come in small packages, and these little pouches are perfect for tiny-sized favors such as flower seed mixes or small candies. By simply cutting out the pattern and scoring the fold lines, a flat sheet of scrapbook paper instantly becomes a three-dimensional container.

one · Copy the template onto a piece of sturdy cardstock at the proper size. Trace around the template onto the back of a piece of cardstock glitter paper. Trace the score lines onto the paper as well. Cut out the box with scissors. Go over the score lines with a stylus or a bone folder.

two · Begin to fold the box along the score lines.

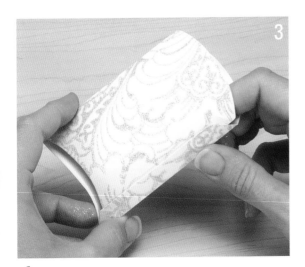

three · Glue the narrow flap on the side of the box in place.

four · Fold the flaps on one side of the puffy box closed, and fill it with sweets of your choice. Fold the other end closed, and tie a piece of gold-edged ribbon around the box to secure the flaps closed. Slip a sprig of leaves under the ribbon, and tie the ribbon in a bow to secure it.

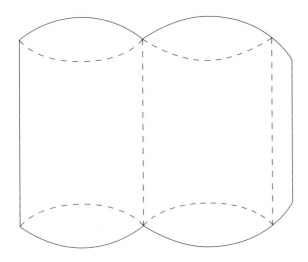

Enlarge box template at 200% to bring it to full size.

pyramid box

MATERIALS

12" (30cm) square printed cardstock

silk leaf

20" (51cm) length of ³/₈" (1cm) wide
message ribbon

stylus, bone folder or embossing tool

Aleene's Tacky Glue

straightedge

pencil

scissors

**Enlarge template at 200%, then
enlarge 125% to bring to full size.**

This pyramid-shaped box is the perfect container for a flower bulb cushioned in shredded paper. With a little water and some sunlight, your guests will enjoy its fragrance and bloom after your wedding. If you prefer a more traditional favor, the pyramid box elegantly accommodates a small stack of chocolate truffles. The pyramid box is a beautifully understated way to package whichever favor you choose.

one · Enlarge the pattern, cut it out and trace it onto the cardstock.

two · With the pattern-side down, use a stylus and a straightedge to score all the dotted fold lines (see Basic Techniques, page 12). Fold up each of the eight small side flaps, and then fold up each of the four points.

three · To connect the points, apply a thin coating of tacky glue to the side flaps and press them together where they meet. Be sure to slide your gift into the pyramid before gluing the flaps of the fourth point.

four · Place the center of the ribbon under the base of the finished pyramid, writing-side down. Bring the ribbon ends up against the sides of the box, so that the writing is visible. Glue the ribbon ends together at the top of the box.

five · Trim the ribbon at an angle and add embellishment, in this instance a silk leaf.

purse box

MATERIALS

12" (30cm) square periwinkle
blue scrapbook paper

cream twisted cord

flat-backed plastic pearl (cabochon)

self-adhesive Velcro dots

Aleene's Tacky glue

stylus, bone folder or embossing tool

straightedge

scissors

pencil

one · Enlarge the pattern, cut it out and trace it onto scrapbook paper. With the pattern-side down, use a stylus and a straightedge to score all the dotted fold lines (see Basic Techniques, page 12).

two · Fold and glue down flap A.

three · Fold each of the scored vertical lines. Fold up the bottom flaps (B, C, D and E).

four · Form the shaped cardstock into a rectangular purse shape. Flaps B and D should fall inside the purse. Glue flap C over flap E to form the bottom of the purse. Glue flap F against the open edge of the purse.

five · Push in the tops of the narrow purse sides. Fold down the top of the purse (flap F).

six · Apply self-adhesive Velcro to the front of the purse and to the underside of flap F.

seven · Glue the pearl cabochon to the front of flap F, positioning it directly over the Velcro.

eight · Glue the cord ends under the bottom edge of flap F.

W ho can resist this charming paper purse? These little bags are sure to dress up your reception tables. Their narrow size makes them ideal for low-profile favors like notepapers, postcards and pens.

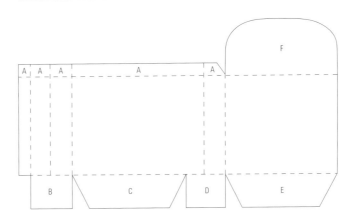

**Enlarge template at
200%, then enlarge 175%
to bring to full size.**

silver leaf box

MATERIALS

4½" x 3¼" x 2½" (11cm x 8cm x 6cm)
blank box

2½" (6cm) wide strip of silver
textured paper (Provo Craft)

4½" x 3¼" (11cm x 8cm) rectangle of
metallic script vellum paper (Colorbök)

silver leaf (Black Ink)

Aleene's Tacky Glue

double-sided tape

scissors

These gilded boxes are perfectly sized to accommodate tea bags or cookie favors. Save money by buying the favors in bulk, and the handmade boxes will bring elegance to their presentation. Create a tabletop centerpiece by stacking them together into a tiered arrangement, or place them individually at each place setting. Long after the contents are devoured, these beautiful boxes are sure to be saved.

one · Cut a 2½" (6cm) wide piece of silver crinkly textured paper, or measure your box and cut a piece of paper to fit around three sides. Apply glue to three sides of the small favor box (two long sides and one short side). Adhere the silver paper to the box. Cut a small 2½" (6cm) wide piece of silver crinkle paper, and glue it onto the remaining uncovered side of the box.

two · Adhere a rectangle of metallic script vellum paper to the box lid (4½" x 3¼" [11cm x 8cm] for this box) with double-sided tape. If your box is a different size, measure and cut a piece of paper to fit.

three · Apply some double-sided tape down the center of a silver leaf, and adhere it to the top center of the vellum rectangle.

GOLD LEAF BOX

• THIS SQUARE BOX IS LARGE ENOUGH to accommodate four brownies. Make this gold box in the same way as the silver box, but add a ribbon embellishment instead of a leaf.

Trace around the box lid onto gold textured paper, cut it out and glue it over the top of the box lid. Then cut 12" (30cm) lengths of gold-printed ribbon, and use double-sided tape to secure one end of each piece of ribbon to the middle inside of the box top. Bring the free ends of the ribbon up over the top of the box lid and tie them into a bow.

magnetic frame place card

MATERIALS

small magnetic wood frames

satin fabric scraps

fusible interfacing

light yellow and green scrapbook paper

metal heart embellishment

Aleene's Platinum Bond Glass &
Bead Glue

computer and printer

iron

scissors

pencil or pen

tip > If you have some-
one sewing your dress or
your bridesmaids' dresses,
save the fabric scraps and
use them under the printed
name cards.

These framed place cards add elegance to reception tables while guiding guests to their seats. Once the meal is over, these personal favors will be enjoyed at home or at work where the magnet will beautifully keep track of stray notes and photos.

1

one · Lay the interfacing on the back side of the scrap of fabric you choose (follow package instructions). Iron the interfacing onto the fabric to adhere it. Lay the cardboard backing from the frame on top of the fabric, and trace around it. Cut out the fabric rectangle.

2

3

two · Print each guest's name onto coordinating scrapbook paper, and cut out a rectangle around the name. Layer the cutout name onto another piece of coordinating scrapbook paper.

three · Layer the fabric piece on top of the cardboard rectangle, and place the name and the plastic cover on top. Slide the layered pieces into the frame.

4

four · Add a gold charm to the outside of the frame, securing it with Aleene's Platinum Bond Glass & Bead glue.

ANOTHER SIMPLY BEAUTIFUL IDEA

Simplify the project by replacing the fabric background with patterned scrapbook paper. In this case, I chose a paper that features a collage of vintage images paired with a lighter wood frame.

rice roses

MATERIALS

5½" x 9" (14cm x 23cm) violet satin fabric folded in half lengthwise to 2¾" x 9" (7cm x 23cm)

6" (15cm) green wood floral picks with wire

wired floral leaves

green floral tape

violet thread

birdseed or other confetti alternative such as heart-shaped puffed rice (Darice)

sewing machine

scissors

*tip > Customize the color of the fabric flowers to match your wedding, and fill your flowers with a favorite confetti alternative—birdseed is a popular and inexpensive choice.

These beautiful roses aren't just decorations; they've been carefully filled with puffed rice hearts. Once the center of the rose is pulled open, a simple flick of the wrist will shower the newlyweds with a cascade of good fortune as they emerge from the chapel.

one · Make sure the piece of violet fabric is folded in half lengthwise with right sides facing each other (it should now measure 2¾ x 9" [7cm x 23cm]). Using violet thread, sew a seam about ½" (1cm) in from the cut edge. Do not sew across the top or bottom.

two · Turn the violet satin tube right-side out.

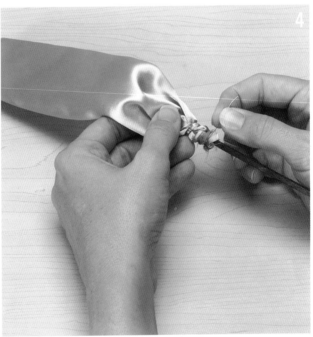

three · Insert a green floral stick into one of the open ends of the fabric tube. Scrunch the fabric around the floral stick, leaving the wire end uncovered.

four · Wrap the wire around the outside of the purple fabric to secure the bottom of the rose.

five · Cover the wire-wrapped fabric with green floral tape.

six · Attach a wired leaf to the base of the flower, over the floral tape.

seven · Pour some heart-shaped puffed rice into the flower (or use birdseed or other confetti of your choice).

eight · Scrunch the fabric down, and shape it into a rose.

ultra-simple favors

WEDDING ORNAMENTS

MATERIALS

WEDDING ORNAMENTS

2" (5cm) crackle-finish glass balls

white paint markers

organdy ribbon

¼" (6mm) wide white satin ribbon

flower embellishments
(The Card Connection,
Hirschberg Schutz & Co.)

Aleene's Platinum Bond
Glass & Bead Glue

scissors

**CANDIED
ALMOND FAVORS**

white patterned fabric

light purple tulle circles

ribbon

gold bells and wedding
ring charms (Darice)

candied almonds

scissors

CANDIED ALMOND FAVORS

Simple favors often add just the right touch to reception tables. Custom-made for a Christmas wedding, personalized glass balls make treasured favors. Or wrap candied almonds in circles of printed lace and tulle. Guests can munch on the crunchy candies that traditionally symbolize the mingled bitterness and sweetness of marriage.

To make these simple wedding ornaments, buy ball ornaments with a crackle finish, and print a sentiment onto one or both sides with a white paint marker. Then glue on a paper flower embellishment, and tie on a sheer ribbon hanger and a coordinating white satin bow.

Cut out a circle of white patterned fabric, and lay a light purple tulle circle on top of it. Simply place some candied almonds in the middle, and gather the fabric up around the sweets. Tie a length of coordinating ribbon and a wedding bell charm around the gathered fabric.

beaded champagne flute lilies

MATERIALS

silver wine charm findings
(Victoria Lynn, Darice)

26-gauge silver wire

pink, crystal and green Japanese seed
beads (or substitute "E" beads)

12 clear glass teardrop beads

2 tan glass teardrop beads

wire cutters

round-nose pliers

tip > Match the beaded
flowers to your wedding
flowers by changing the bead
colors or by shaping the
beaded wire into rounded or
teardrop petals.

Poised at your fingertips and filled with bubbling champagne, these elegantly trimmed flutes are worthy of a lifetime of celebratory toasts. The shimmering lilies will drink up the flash and sparkle of the spotlight all through your reception. In the event that one of the glasses breaks, rest assured the flower will simply slip onto a new glass.

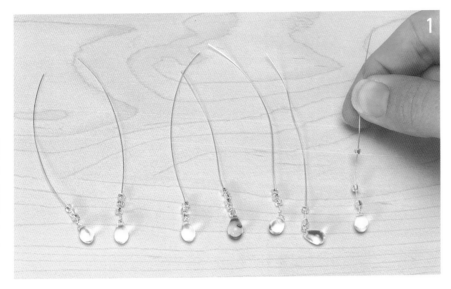

one · Cut seven 3½" (9cm) lengths of wire for the flower's stamen. Thread a wire with a clear teardrop bead so it rests ½" (1cm) from the end. Fold the small wire end down and twist the wire around the long end of the wire to secure the bead in place. Repeat for five other wire pieces. For the center stamen, thread on a tan teardrop bead, and secure it. Thread five crystal beads onto each wire.

two · Use round-nose pliers to wrap the wire ends around the base of the stamens to form a loop. The loop should be big enough to slide onto the hoop. Cut off the tails with wire cutters.

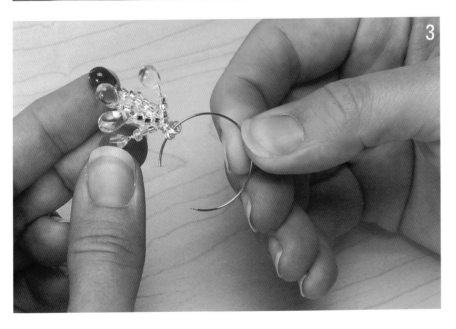

three · Slide the loop of the stamen grouping onto the silver wire hoop.

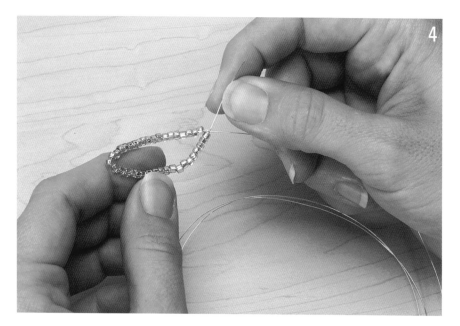

four · Cut a long piece of silver wire and thread 34 pink Japanese seed beads onto one end of it. Wrap the short end of the wire around the base of the beads to create the first petal.

five · Continue to make pink beaded petals, looping them over each other to build a layered circular flower.

six · Finish making the flower petals (eight total). Wrap the petals around the base of the beaded stamen wires. Wrap the flower wire ends around the loop you made in the stamen.

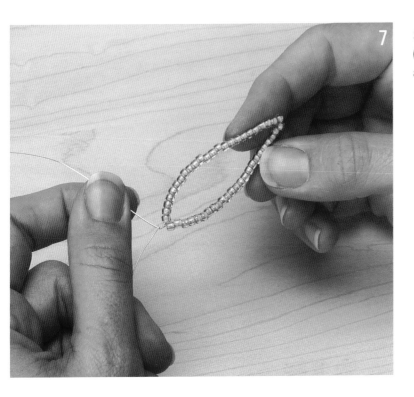

seven · Thread 48 green Japanese seed beads onto a 12" (30cm) length of wire, and fold the beaded wire in half to shape a pointed leaf. Twist the wires several times to secure the leaf.

eight · Thread 21 Japanese seed beads onto one of the wires to make the vein in the leaf. Run the newly beaded wire up the center of the leaf, and wrap it around the pointed leaf end to secure it in place. Trim the vein wire end, but leave the stem end intact to join the leaf to the flower.

nine · Attach the leaf underneath the beaded petals by tightly wrapping the stem wire around the petal wires. Bend up the very end of the wire hoop with pliers so that it will slide into the hole on the hoop to secure the charm to the champagne flute.

correspondence
& keepsakes

On a shelf in my closet is a box filled with keepsakes from our wedding that I bring down once in a while to share with the kids. They're always surprised to see what Mom and Dad looked like when they were young. Long after the boys lose interest, I sit on the bed turning the pages of our wedding album, reading the cards and the wedding program, and feeling incredibly blessed to have met Jon.

From the first engagement announcement, the paper waterfall begins with wedding shower invitations and ends in a pool of thank you notes after the ceremony. In this chapter, you'll find ways to chronicle your wedding by using all the special pieces of paper created around the occasion. Incorporate cards, programs, menus and hotel brochures into your keepsakes to record the well-wishes of friends and family. Wedding photographs are the favorite way to reminisce, so take the time to frame the pictures you want to display in your home, and organize other photos in albums. You don't need to invest in elaborate albums or guest books—look for plain versions to personalize. Consider creating miniature albums for family or even for wedding favors.

In addition to all the cards you receive in celebration of your wedding, you might make one or two handmade ones to give away. If you find a design that speaks to your relationship, create one for your fiancé and enclose a heartfelt note. He'll appreciate your thoughts during the flurry of preparations.

CHAPTER

2

47

card cake

MATERIALS

6½" (17cm) wide x 3¼" (8cm) tall round-lidded papier mâché box

7½" (19cm) wide x 4" (10cm) tall round-lidded papier mâché box

three pink and white silk hydrangea stems

¾" (2cm) wide pink grosgrain ribbon

1" (3cm) wide white grosgrain ribbon

white and pink quartz acrylic paint (Delta)

hot glue gun and melt sticks

wire cutters

craft knife

paintbrush

scissors

pencil

tip > If you're having a large wedding, you may consider increasing the size of the cake to accommodate more cards. Select a larger hatbox to add another tier to the base of the cake. To enable the cards to fall through to the bottom layer, you'll need to cut openings in the base of the second box and in the top of the new box.

Skip the flour and eggs—this no-bake wedding cake is made with two cardboard hatboxes. Paint the boxes white and pink, wrap them in ribbon and frost the confection with silk flowers. Stack them together to create a two-tiered cake that never needs refrigeration. Display the finished cake on the gift table, where it will serve not only as a beautiful centerpiece, but also as a clever receptacle for gift cards.

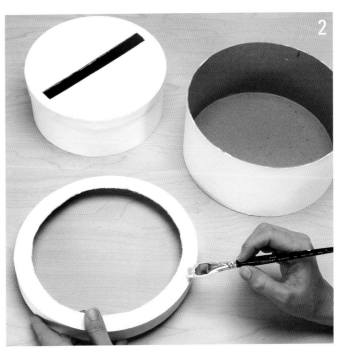

one · Place the small box on top of the large box, centering it on top of the box lid. Trace around the bottom of the small box with a pencil. Cut the top of the big box lid along the pencil line with a craft knife. Trace a ¾" x 6" (2cm x 15cm) slot onto the center of the small box lid. Use a sharp craft knife to cut out the slot for the cards, and then cut the bottom off the small box.

two · Paint all four pieces white (the big box and its lid ring, and the small box and its lid with slot). Apply a second coat of white paint. Allow the paint to dry.

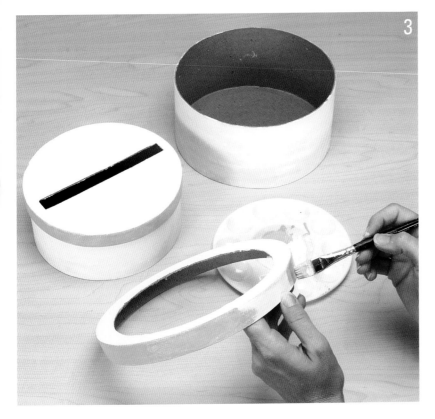

three · Use two shades of pink (one darker and one lighter) to drybrush in some color around the bottom of the big box and the bottom of the small box. Paint the rim of both the small box lid and the big box lid solid pink. Apply another coat of paint if necessary. Allow the paint to dry.

four · Apply hot glue around the cut opening in the lid of the bottom box. Position the base of the small box into the glue.

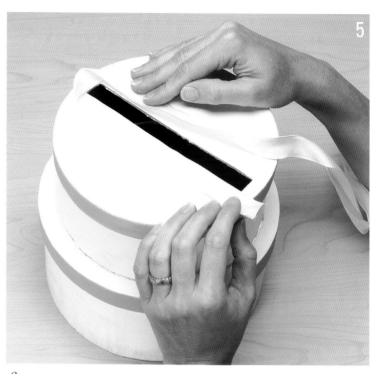

five · Line the slot on the top of the card cake with pink ribbon, securing it with hot glue.

six · Cut hydrangea blooms off their stems with wire cutters and hot glue them around the top of the box and around the first tier of the cake.

seven · Glue a piece of white grosgrain ribbon around the center of each layer of cake. Fold a flat, looped bow with another piece of grosgrain ribbon, and glue it to the front center of the cake.

ribbon and ring photo album

MATERIALS

4¾" x 6½" (12cm x 17cm) mini photo album (holds 36 4"x 6" [10cm x 15cm] photos)

two sheets of printed scrapbook paper (Chateau Swag flat paper, K&Company) trimmed to 4½" x 6⅛" (11cm x 16cm)

¾" (2cm) wide double-faced satin ribbon (Anna Griffin)

¼" (6mm) wide cream grosgrain ribbon

silver ring charm (Making Memories)

computer and printer

double-sided tape

Aleene's Tacky glue

Aleene's Platinum Bond Glass & Bead Glue

hot glue gun and melt sticks

scissors

This little album makes an ideal gift for the parents of the bride and groom. It's small enough to fit in a handbag, making it an ideal brag book to share wedding photographs with friends. Printed scrapbook endpapers, satin ribbon and a charm quickly spiff up the inexpensive album and transform it into a unique personalized keepsake.

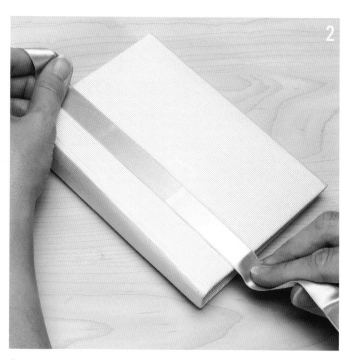

one · Print your names and your wedding date onto patterned paper of your choice, and trim the paper to fit inside the front cover of a premade mini photo album (4½" x 6⅛" [11cm x 16cm] for this album). Make sure to print the dates and names in the left bottom center of the paper, and glue it to the inside front cover. Glue another piece of paper the same size to the back inside cover of the album.

two · Apply a line of double-sided tape to the front of the album, and adhere a piece of ribbon that coordinates with the endpaper onto the front of the album.

three · Wrap the ends of the ribbon to the inside of the book, and adhere them with double-sided tape so that the ends overlap.

four · Cut a small length of cream ribbon, and tie it in a bow around a silver ring charm. Glue the tied charm onto the top of the ribbon on the front of the album with Aleene's Platinum Bond Glass & Bead Glue.

mini wedding album

light purple photo album

light purple patterned scrapbook paper

paper embellishments
(Jolene's Boutique)

computer and printer

double-sided tape

scissors

tip > You might consider slipping your wedding program inside the first couple of photo sleeves and have the albums ready for the ushers to present to your guests as they take their seats before the ceremony.

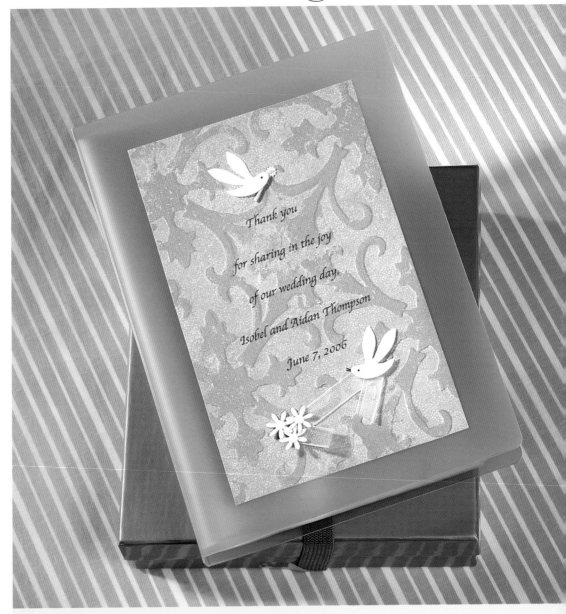

Thank you

for sharing in the joy

of our wedding day,

Isobel and Aidan Thompson

June 7, 2006

Small albums come in all shapes and sizes, and this light plastic variety is widely available and inexpensive, making it ideal to distribute as a wedding favor. Instead of tucking your printed wedding announcement inside the front cover, trim it and mount it directly over the center of the front cover with double-sided tape. Apply a pair of self-adhesive paper doves to the top and bottom of the paper to frame the wording.

love letters album

MATERIALS

8¾" x 6" (22cm x 15cm) album (C.R. Gibson)

double mat board set: picture size 3½" x 5" (9cm x 13cm), opening size 3" x 4½" (8cm x 11cm)

¼" (6mm) wide blue satin ribbon

1" (3cm) wide gold organdy ribbon (Offray)

1½" (4cm) wide gold luminous organdy ribbon

antique gold square alphabet tiles (JoAnn Essentials)

double-sided tape

Aleene's Platinum Bond Glass & Bead Glue

scissors

Don't hide all your favorite wedding photographs inside your album. This customized album beautifully displays a special photograph on the cover, allowing you to enjoy the image more often. The frame is cleverly created from two layers of ribbon-covered mat board mounted directly onto the cover of a purchased album.

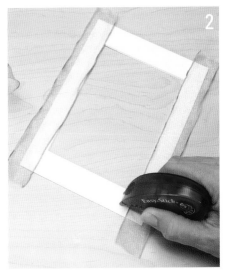

one · Buy a precut two-piece mat board that fits on the front of your photo album with a small border around it. Cut four pieces of narrow blue satin ribbon, two 5½" (14cm) lengths and two 4" (10cm) lengths. Use double-sided tape to adhere the ribbons to the edges of the mat board, overlapping the ribbons at the corners.

two · Cut two 8" (20cm) lengths of gold organdy ribbon. Use double-sided tape to adhere the ribbon to the long sides of the mat board.

three · Cut two more pieces of gold organdy ribbon, and adhere them to the short sides of the mat board so they overlap with the first two ribbons at the corners. Wrap the ends of the ribbons around to the back of the mat board, and secure them with double-sided tape.

four · Apply double-sided tape to the back of the bottom mat board, and lay the picture on the front center of the album and the mat board on top of the picture. Apply double-sided tape to the back of the top mat board, and press it on top of the first mat board.

five · Cut a 8" to 10" (20cm to 25cm) length of sheer gold luminous organdy ribbon, and tie it around the cover of the album.

six · Adhere letters to spell *Love* on the mat board with Aleene's glue.

here comes the bride card

MATERIALS

5" x 7" (13cm x 18cm) blank
white card and envelope

white and off-white cardstock

small white flowers (Darice)

small white feather

rub-on message (Making Memories)

black and red fine-tipped markers

double-sided tape

glue stick

hot glue gun and melt sticks

scissors

pencil

ANOTHER SIMPLY
BEAUTIFUL
IDEA

H ere comes the bride, all dressed in white…this card,
featuring a bride with a classic bob hairstyle and
luscious red lipstick, is reminiscent of the roaring
twenties. She's wearing a classic white dress simply accented
with a flowing feather and a modest bouquet of miniature
silk bridal flowers.

**Create a more colorful version of this card, and send it as a thank you note to your bridesmaids.
Or use it as an invitation to a bridesmaids' luncheon. To make the bridesmaid, copy the pattern
on page 127.**

one · Remove the protective sheet from the word you choose. Place the rub-on word sheet firmly in place over the spot on the front of the card where you'd like the word to go. Holding the rub-on sheet firmly in place, rub over it with the supplied stick, working from one end to the other. Lift the sheet off to make sure the word transferred completely. If not, lay the sheet down again, and continue to rub. Peel up the sheet when the transfer is complete.

two · Copy the body pattern on page 124 onto a piece of sturdy cardstock, and cut it out. Make sure to draw on the face as well. Trace the bride's silhouette on page 124 onto a piece of off-white cardstock. Use a fine-tipped black marker to draw on the face and hair. Add red lips with a fine-tipped red marker. Using double-sided tape, adhere the bride to the front center of the card above the rub-on word.

three · Copy the wedding dress pattern and the headband pattern on page 124 at the proper size. Make a template from the copy. Trace the wedding dress and the headband onto white cardstock, and cut them out. Adhere them onto the bride's silhouette with a glue stick.

four · Hot glue flowers into the bride's hand, and hot glue a small white feather to the side of her headband.

tip > Use a foam spacer to add dimension by lifting the dress off the card.

lovebird pop-up card

MATERIALS

4¼" x 5½" (11cm x 14cm) pearl card and envelope

2½" x 4⅛" (6cm x 11cm) ivory art paper with silver and gold flecks

vellum message trimmed to 1¼" x 2¼" (3cm x 6cm) (JoAnn Essentials)

cream-and-white patterned scrapbook paper

cardstock

gold heart embellishment

gold paint marker

black fine-tipped marker

double-sided tape

Aleene's Memory Glue

glue stick

scissors

pencil

Lovebirds are locked in a heart-shaped embrace as they cleverly pop up from the center of this card. This hand-made card makes a perfect keepsake to give to your fiancé or to make for newlywed friends. Beautifully original, it will inevitably find its way into a wedding scrapbook where it will be enjoyed for years to come.

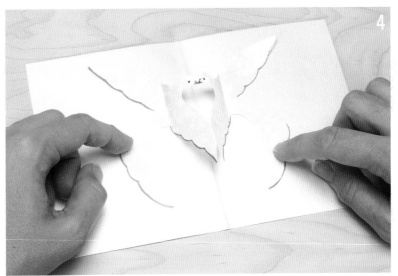

one · Trace the bird pattern on page 125 onto a piece of cardstock to make a template. Fold a piece of silver-and-gold patterned paper in half. Place the bird template on top of the folded paper with the beak exactly flush against the fold. Trace around the template with a pencil. Keep the paper folded and cut the bird out, making sure the paper halves remain connected at the beak.

two · Unfold the lovebirds and add gold highlights along the beak, wing and tail edges with a gold paint marker. Use a fine-tipped black marker to give the lovebirds eyes.

three · Following the dotted line on the template, fold back the top portion of the wing on each bird.

four · Apply glue with a glue stick to the folded portion of the birds' wings and tails, leaving the other areas free of glue so they can pop up. Fold the cardstock piece in half to make the card base. Position the birds over the inside center of the card so the connected beaks fall exactly into the center crease.

five · To create the front of the card, glue a 2½" x 4⅛" (6cm x 11cm) piece of cream flecked paper onto the center front of the card. Layer on a vellum message cut to 1¼" x 2¼" (3cm x 6cm) and adhere it with double-sided tape. To finish, glue a small gold heart charm onto the bottom of the layered squares with Aleene's Memory Glue.

bride's shower card

MATERIALS

tag cards

2⅝" x 3⅝" (7cm x 9cm) white plaid vellum (Colorbök)

self-stick silver glitter paper (Darice)

white floral wire

three small white satin roses (Darice)

¼" (6mm) wide sheer iridescent ribbon

message stamp (Anna Griffin)

black inkpad

double-sided tape

hot glue gun and melt sticks

wire cutters

scissors

pencil

The umbrella has always been the traditional symbol for a wedding shower. This updated icon breaks out from under the rain clouds and takes on a sun-drenched appearance as it sparkles with glitter and blooms miniature roses. It takes only minutes to assemble multiples of this shower invitation on purchased tag-shaped cards.

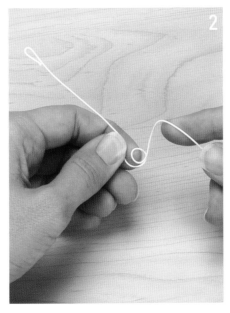

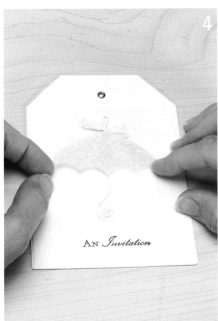

one · Use double-sided tape to adhere the 2⅝" x 3⅝" (7cm x 9cm) rectangle of white plaid vellum paper to the front center of the card. Stamp the words *An Invitation* below the vellum square with black ink.

two · Cut a 6" (15cm) piece of white floral wire with wire cutters. Twist the bottom of the wire piece into a spiral, and bend down the top ¼" (6mm) portion of the wire.

three · Cut a small piece of sheer iridescent ribbon, and tie it in a bow around the wire just below the doubled-over top part of wire.

four · Lay the wire piece onto the front center of the card where you'd like the center of the umbrella to be. Copy the umbrella pattern on this page to the proper size. Trace the umbrella onto a piece of silver glitter sticker paper, and cut it out. Simply peel the backing off the umbrella, and adhere it to the card on top of the wire piece so the sticker holds the wire in place.

five · Snip three miniature white roses off their wire stems with wire cutters, and hot glue them in a row to the bottom of the umbrella. Cut a piece of sheer ribbon, tie a knot in the center, and pull both ends of the ribbon out through the grommet hole at the top of the card. The knot will prevent the center of the ribbon from pulling all the way out.

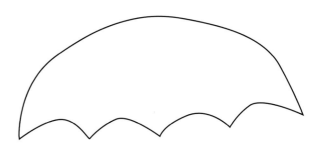

Umbrella template shown at actual size.

stitched flowers invitation

MATERIALS

blue cardstock

white cardstock

green cardstock

silk flower

rhinestones

thread

Aleene's Memory Glue

computer and printer

sewing machine

straightedge

stylus, bone folder or embossing tool

scissors

pencil

Joanna Dower
&
Matthew Masterson

together with our parents
William and Jacquelyn Dower & Vincent and Pamela Masterson
request the pleasure of your company as we celebrate our marriage on
Saturday, July 30, two thousand and five at
five-thirty in the afternoon

Omni Hotel
676 N. Michigan Avenue
Chicago, Illinois
reception to follow

S titched stems blooming with miniature silk flowers vine around this unique wedding invitation. Miniature rhinestones add sparkle to each flower center. Slip the finished invitation into a folded cardstock sleeve for a formal presentation. Your creative handmade wedding invitation will surely foster excitement for the upcoming celebration.

ANOTHER SIMPLY BEAUTIFUL IDEA

While you have the sewing machine at the ready, create a matching set of thank you notes to coordinate with your invitations. This pink version uses the same color cardstock as the invitation sleeve. Cut it to a standard note card size, score and fold it in half. Machine stitch flower stems over the front of the card, then glue petals, rhinestones and leaves onto the stems.

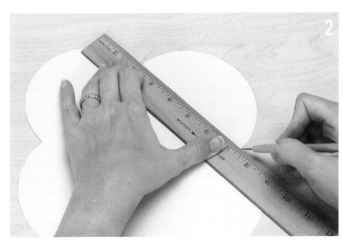

one · Copy the petal sleeve on page 127 to the proper size, and cut it out to make a template. Trace the pattern onto a piece of blue cardstock, and cut it out with scissors.

two · Use a straightedge and a stylus to score the dotted lines on the pattern onto the cardstock.

three · Print the invitation on a piece of quality white cardstock. Stitch several curvy stems on the card around the typed message. Pick a thread color that complements the color of your cardstock and the color of your petal sleeve. I chose blue thread to match the blue cardstock sleeve. Apply a little glue to the end of each stitched stem to secure the thread.

four · Pull apart the petals from a silk flower and glue a flower at the top of each stem using Aleene's Memory Glue.

five · Glue a rhinestone in the center of each flower.

six · Cut out two small green leaves from a piece of cardstock. Glue the leaves in places that accent the stems and flowers. Fold the blue petal envelope around the invitation.

layer cake guest book

MATERIALS

7½" x 5¾" (19cm x 15cm) purchased
guest book (C.R. Gibson)

2¾" x 3¼" (7cm x 8cm)
matte silver paper

2⅝" x 3" (7cm x 8cm) white cardstock

21¼" x 2¾" (6cm x 7cm)
striped silver paper

textured or flocked white paper

white-dotted vellum

string of pearls (Darice)

silk flowers with pearl center

1⅝" (4cm) length of ¼" (6mm)
wide white grosgrain ribbon

⅞" (2cm) wide white organdy ribbon

double-sided tape

hot glue gun and melt sticks

wire cutters

scissors

pencil

tip > If cake isn't your cup of tea, consider mounting a favorite manufactured scrapbook embellishment on top of the background squares.

Crafting your own guest book is a piece of cake. Save pennies by purchasing a plain, blank guest book, and personalize it with layers of cut scrapbook paper and vellum sheets. Small lengths of pearls and a single bridal flower decorate the finished cake. Don't underestimate the value of a traditional guest book—years from now you'll enjoy flipping through the volume of signatures and well-wishes.

one · Cut out three pieces of scrapbook paper in coordinating shades. Adhere the largest piece, a 2¾" x 3¼" (6cm x 8cm) rectangle of matte silver paper, to the center of the guest book with double-sided tape. Layer the other two pieces of paper (a 2⅝" x 3" [7cm x 8cm] piece of white cardstock and a 2¼" x 2¾" [6cm x 7cm] piece of striped silver paper) on top of the large one, and adhere them with double-sided tape.

two · Trace the cake layers pattern on page 127 onto a piece of cardstock to make a template. Trace around the template onto white flocked paper and cut out the cake layers. Hot glue the cake layers on top of the layered paper squares. Trace the middle layer of cake onto a piece of white-dotted vellum paper and cut it out. Glue it directly on top of the second flocked layer of cake.

three · Cut a small piece of white grosgrain ribbon to fit along the bottom layer of cake. Glue it down with a hot glue gun. Glue on small pieces of pearl trim "icing" between the layers of cake with a hot glue gun.

four · Tie a piece of sheer white ribbon into a bow, and hot glue it over the grosgrain white ribbon. Cut a silk flower off its stem, and hot glue it to the top of the cake to finish.

accessories

Before designing the projects for this book, I scoured stores and current publications, researching trends and looking at what people were buying for their weddings. I was surprised by how saturated the market was with plain white ring pillows, flower girl baskets and hair accessories, when the fashion magazines were filled with color. I've added vibrant accents of color to many of the projects in this section.

You can customize any of these pieces to your own color scheme. For example, coordinate the silk flowers in the headband with those used along the top edge of the basket to make a perfectly turned-out flower girl. You may also use beads that match your bridesmaids' dresses to make the hair combs in this chapter. You can even create a color-coordinated ring pillow for the smallest gentleman in the bridal party.

Most of the projects require little or no sewing experience. In many cases, silk flowers are simply pulled apart and glued into place. The flowered shawl is an ideal beginning sewing machine project, and the ring bearer's pillow requires a bit of sewing know-how or the help of a sewing-savvy friend. Whether you make just one project from this chapter or many, your handmade accessories are sure to garner compliments from your wedding guests.

CHAPTER

3

flower girl headband

MATERIALS

silk-covered headband
(Hirschberg Schutz & Co.)

silk flowers: white baby's breath,
pink delphinium spray,
purple star-shaped flowers,
green flower buds

3mm round rhinestones (Darice)

hot glue gun and melt sticks

wire cutters

tip > If smaller hair accessories better fit the needs of your wedding party, use platinum bond glue to attach silk flowers with rhinestone centers to barrette backs and hair combs.

This crown of blooming flowers will keep stray hairs out of your flower girl's eyes so everyone can see her face as she comes down the aisle. To customize the headband, simply select flowers and rhinestones that coordinate with her dress and your floral color scheme. The finished hair accessory easily slides into brushed hair, sparing both mother and child hours of styling at the hair salon.

one · Cut five pink flowers off their stems with wire cutters, and hot glue them onto the white headband, spacing them evenly.

two · Cut lots of white flowers off their stems with wire cutters, and hot glue them all around the pink flowers to cover the surface of the headband. Leave the last two inches on each side of the headband uncovered.

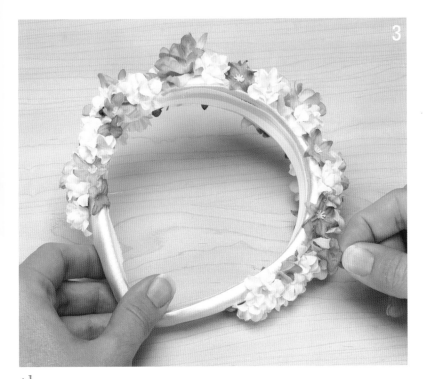

three · Glue seven purple flowers and six green flower buds on each side of the headband.

four · For added sparkle, hot glue clear rhinestones on the center of each colored flower.

flower girl basket

MATERIALS

wicker basket 5" (13cm) high and
9" (23cm) wide at top (18" [46cm]
wide at base)

1½" (4cm) wide wired
blue ribbon (Offray)

9½" x 24" (24cm x 61cm) light
blue fabric

three stems of purple-blue
silk hydrangeas

hot glue gun and melt sticks

wire cutters

scissors

tip > Add fabric and flowers to smaller baskets, and then fill them with wedding favors to create charming tabletop centerpieces.

Flowers, fabric and ribbon quickly add a rich blend of textures to a modern leather-handled wicker basket. Easily assembled in advance of the wedding, this blooming basket is guaranteed never to wilt. The clusters of silk hydrangeas are firmly glued in place, making the finished basket sturdy enough to withstand accidental drops and spills.

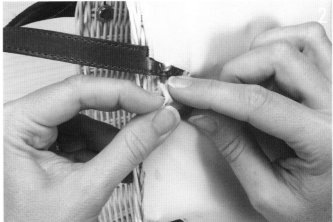

one • Fold a piece of 9½" x 24" (24cm x 61cm) blue lightweight fabric in half lengthwise. Hot glue the fabric to an oval wicker basket, keeping the folded edge at the bottom of the basket. Where the ends of the fabric overlap, fold under the raw edge of the fabric to create a seam, and glue it down.

two • Use small scissors to cut a ½" (1cm) slit in the fabric at the base of each leather handle. Fold the cut edges under and hot glue them to the basket on either side of the handles.

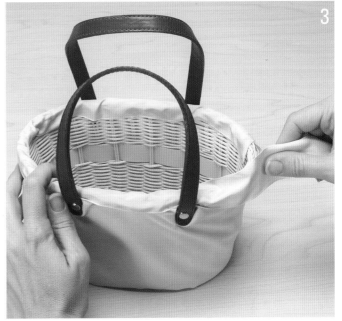

three • Using a hot glue gun and melt sticks, adhere the 1½" (4cm) wide wired blue ribbon to the top of the wicker basket by folding it in half, so half the ribbon is on the outside of the basket concealing the raw fabric edge and the other half is on the inside.

four • Cut silk flowers off their stems with wire cutters, and hot glue them along the border of the purse.

five • Cut an 8" (20cm) length of ribbon, and tie it in a bow around the handles.

*tip > Place a lace handkerchief inside the basket before filling it with petals.

ring bearer's pillow

MATERIALS

10" x 10" (25cm x 25cm) square of white satin

10" x 10" (25cm x 25cm) square of patterned cotton

45" (114cm) of 2⅛" (5cm) wide green satin ribbon

four ⅜" (1cm) wide pearl hook buttons

four ¾" (2cm) wide green toggle buttons

white organdy ribbon (for tying on rings)

fiber fill

white thread

sewing needle

tapestry needle

sewing machine

straight pins

straightedge

scissors

ANOTHER SIMPLY BEAUTIFUL IDEA

The key to tying the different elements of your pillow together is to coordinate the ribbon and buttons with the dominant color in the more vibrant of your two fabrics.

This elegantly tailored pillow is the ideal way to show-case two of your favorite wedding fabrics. Satin ribbon brings sheen to the sides of the fabric squares, and the tightly embedded toggle buttons add dimension to the stuffed pillow. After the ceremony, remove the organdy ribbon and arrange the pillow alongside your bed linens and decorative pillows where it will add sentiment to your bedroom décor.

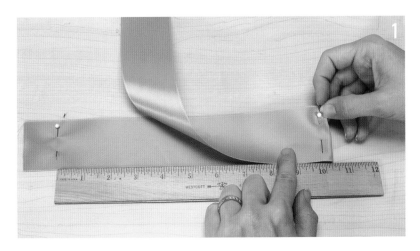

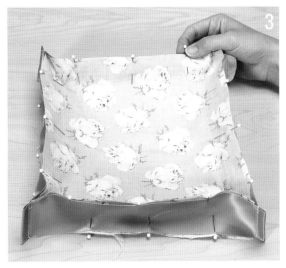

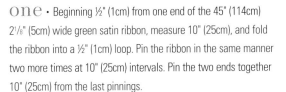

one · Beginning ½" (1cm) from one end of the 45" (114cm) 2⅛" (5cm) wide green satin ribbon, measure 10" (25cm), and fold the ribbon into a ½" (1cm) loop. Pin the ribbon in the same manner two more times at 10" (25cm) intervals. Pin the two ends together 10" (25cm) from the last pinnings.

two · Sew seams at each pinned interval to make the corners of the ring pillow.

three · Place the square of 10" x 10" (25cm x 25cm) white satin fabric right-side up on your work surface, and place the square of patterned cotton fabric right-side down on top of it. Pin the ribbon to both pieces of fabric, with the right side of the ribbon facing inward (all right sides should be facing each other).

four · Sew all the pieces together with individual straight seams, stopping at each corner. Leave a 2" (5cm) opening along the center of one side for stuffing.

five · Use the 2" (5cm) opening to turn the pillow right-side out.

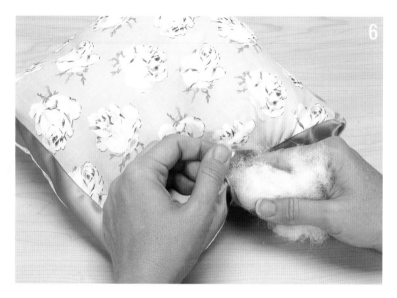 6

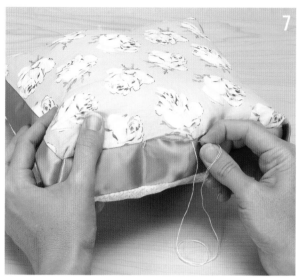 7

 8

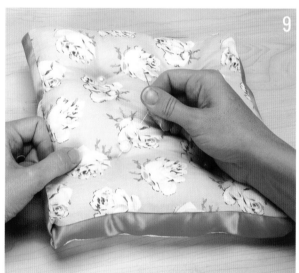 9

six · Insert fiber fill into the opening in the pillow, filling the corners first. The top and bottom of the pillow should be fairly flat—be careful not to fill the pillow too full.

seven · Use a sewing needle and thread to hand-sew the 2" (5cm) opening closed.

eight · Choose two different kinds of buttons—I chose green toggle buttons and pearl hook buttons. Thread a needle and sew the first green toggle button on the top side of the pillow about 2½" (6cm) diagonally in from one corner.

nine · Bring the needle down through the pillow and sew on a pearl hook button directly under the green toggle button on the other side of the pillow. Pull the thread tightly to embed both buttons in the pillow. Sew up and down through both buttons several times to secure them. Sew on three more buttons 2½" (6cm) diagonally in from the remaining three corners.

ten · Thread a 12" (30cm) piece of white organdy ribbon onto a tapestry needle, and make a single stitch to attach it to the front center of the pillow. Thread the rings through one ribbon end and then trap them in the bow.

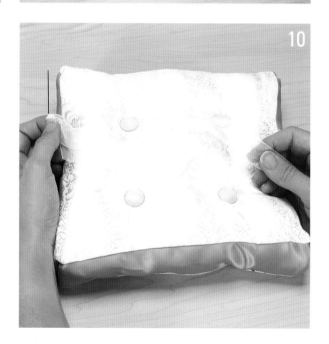 10

white rose bouquet

tip > Switch silver charms for framed prints, selecting personalized tokens that symbolize your relationship and wedding day. After the wedding, have a jeweler place the charms on a chain bracelet. Consider adding a charm at each anniversary to continue creating a keepsake of your married life.

At first glance, you may mistake this simple arrangement of roses for a traditional wedding bouquet. However, it's really a unique twist on a tried-and-true wedding day staple. The collection of framed photographs suspended from narrow ribbons makes it more meaningful than the standard bouquet. These exquisite miniatures of relatives are an original way to keep those in your heart at your fingertips during your wedding ceremony.

one • Cut the stems off both the cream roses and deep pink roses so they're the same length. Use sharp scissors to cut the thorns and leaves off the trimmed stems. Arrange the flowers into a pleasing bouquet.

two • Secure the stems into a bundle by wrapping them with green floral tape.

three • Cut a 7" (18cm) length of wide yellow ribbon, long enough to reach down one side of the bouquet and up on the other side so that the ends of the stems are covered with ribbon. Secure the ribbon on either top side with corsage pins.

four • Starting at the base of the stems, wrap a second yellow ribbon length around the stems until you reach the top of the stems, just beneath the flowers. When you reach the top, trim the ribbon off the spool, fold the end under and secure with a corsage pin.

five · Tie a third ribbon into a full bow, and trim the ends of the ribbon at decorative angles.

six · Make small photocopies of pictures of family members and friends, and line up the small images on a piece of white paper. Glue the strip of images to the back of a piece of decorative scrapbook paper to create a finished-looking backing for the frames. Lay a tiny charm frame over an image, and cut around it to fit. There is a sticky solution on the back side of the frames, so you will not need to use any extra glue to adhere the image to the frame. Simply press them firmly together to secure them. Repeat for four more images and four more frames.

seven · Tie each frame to a piece of narrow sheer off-white ribbon.

eight · To finish the bouquet, bring all the ribbon ends together, and tie them around the stems just above the bow.

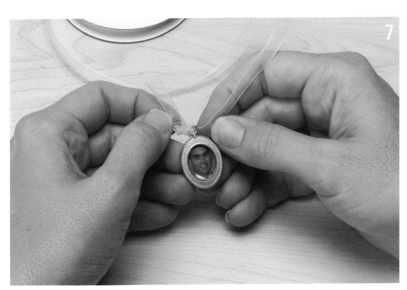

emergency wedding kit

MATERIALS

4½" (11cm) square basket with lid

white acrylic paint (Delta)

metallic silver paint (Delta Gleams)

embroidered card embellishment

white silk bridal flowers

white organdy ribbon

paintbrush

scissors

pencil

tip > If you have trouble locating a basket with a lid, substitute a zippered bag or a decorative metal tin. Just be sure to select a convenient portable container that can be closed to prevent the small contents from spilling out.

Filled with useful items such as bobby pins, clear nail polish and a sewing kit, this little lidded basket makes a perfect wedding shower gift. This practical gift will allow the bride and her wedding party to easily cope with any last-minute wardrobe, cosmetic or hairstyle disasters on her wedding day.

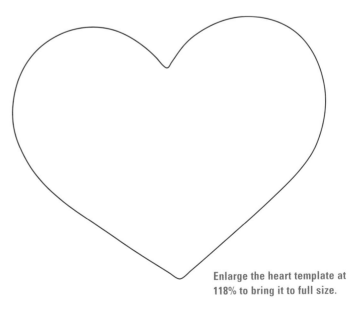

one • Buy a small basket with a lid that closes securely. Paint the top of the basket white with acrylic paint. Apply another coat of paint, if necessary. Allow the paint to dry.

two • Copy the heart template and trace it onto the box top. Paint the heart silver. You may have to apply several coats of silver paint.

three • Adhere the fabric scrapbooking embellishment to the center of the heart. (It has a self-sticking back, so simply press it down to secure it.)

four • Tie a sprig of white flowers to the box handle with a length of wide white organdy ribbon. Fill the basket with any "emergency" supplies the bride might need for her big day.

Enlarge the heart template at 118% to bring it to full size.

antique rose barrette

MATERIALS

3" (8cm) metal barrette backs

¾" x 4¾" (2cm x 12cm) cardstock strip

8" (20cm) of 1" (3cm) wide
ivory grosgrain ribbon

8" (20cm) of 2" (5cm) wide
ivory organdy ribbon

off-white silk flower stem
of small rosebuds

clothespins or an elastic band

Aleene's Platinum Bond Super Fabric
textile glue

Aleene's Tacky Glue

hot glue gun and melt sticks

wire cutters

scissors

ANOTHER SIMPLY BEAUTIFUL IDEA

Create an arrangement of white and ivory buttons by stacking them together across the barrette back. The success of this project hinges on using strong textile glue to anchor the buttons in place.

Layers of ivory ribbon and silk flowers give an antique appearance to these subtle hair accessories. Both inexpensive and quick to make, you'll be surprised that underneath all the trimmings is a humble rectangle cardboard barrette base.

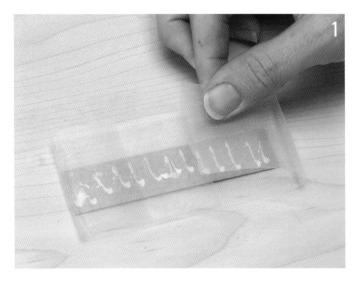

one · Apply tacky glue to the ¾" x 4¾" (2cm x 12cm) piece of cardboard, and adhere an 8" (20cm) length of 2" (5cm) wide organdy ribbon to it, folding the ends of the ribbon over to the back side of the cardstock strip.

two · Cut an 8" (20cm) length of ivory grosgrain ribbon, and use tacky glue to adhere it, wrapping the grosgrain ribbon around the layered cardboard and sheer ribbon with the ends overlapping in the back.

three · Cut off-white roses off their stems with wire cutters. Hot glue the roses along the grosgrain ribbon.

four · Adhere four leaves to the barrette, two on the front sides and two on the back sides.

five · Use textile glue to adhere the decorative top to the metal clip. Clamp with clothespins or wrap with an elastic band while the glue sets.

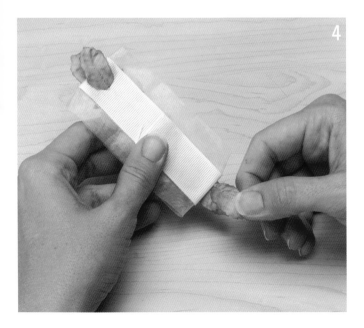

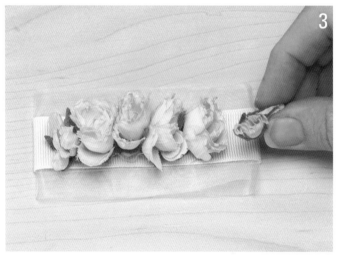

rhinestone flower hair clip

MATERIALS

bobby pins (Hirschberg Schutz & Co.)

purple delphinium silk flower stem

3mm AB Swarovski crystals (Darice)

silver mini marbles (Halcraft)

Aleene's Platinum Bond Glass & Bead Glue

wire cutters

ANOTHER SIMPLY BEAUTIFUL IDEA

The petals on some varieties of silk flowers are sprinkled with clear plastic dewdrops. As these petals already capture the light, it's unnecessary to edge them with mini marbles. This variation uses glistening blue hollyhock petals and a rhinestone center.

B ring an unexpected touch of sparkle and color to your hair with these flowering bobby pins. Silk flowers are simply glued to bobby pins, then the petals are edged with shimmering silver mini marbles, and the last step is to add a Swarovski crystal rhinestone flower center.

one · Cut a purple flower off its stem with wire cutters.

two · Pull the petals of the flower apart so that it is separated into layers (see Basic Techniques, page 13). Apply a dab of Aleene's glue to the round, flat end of the bobby pin, and adhere the bottom petal layer of the flower to it. Apply more glue to the bottom petal layer, and adhere the next layer. Repeat until all the layers have been adhered.

three · Glue a crystal onto the center of the top petal layer.

four · Apply some Aleene's glue to different areas of the petals, making sure to coat some of the edges. Sprinkle silver mini marbles over the glue areas, and shake off any extras.

flower wristband

MATERIALS

9" (23cm) of 1" (3cm) wide
off-white grosgrain ribbon

anemone silk flower stem

light yellow crystal toggle button

⅝" (2cm) silver "D" rings (Darice)

off-white thread

sewing needle

wire cutters

scissors

ANOTHER SIMPLY BEAUTIFUL IDEA

**Pretty in pink, this anemone
wristband adds a blush of
color to your ensemble.
Not just for formal occasions,
this technique can also be
used to make a casual watch-
band. Simply switch to a patterned ribbon, cut the length
in half and sew a half to each
side of the watch face. Skip
the flower and use "D" rings
to fasten the two ribbon ends
together.**

Don't want to be weighed down by a cumbersome old-fashioned wrist corsage? Try this updated light-weight flowering wristband instead. The adjustable strap lets it wrap snugly around your wrist so it stays in place all night long, keeping your hands free for an evening of celebrating and dancing.

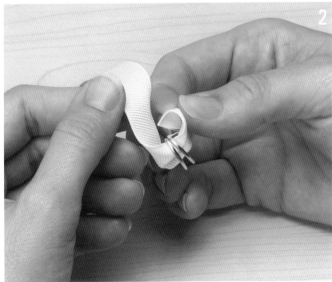

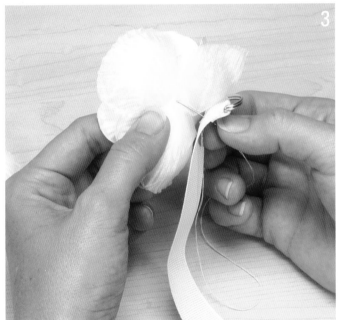

one · Cut a cream flower off its stem with wire cutters. Pull the plastic center out and separate the petals (see Basic Techniques, page 13).

two · Slide two "D" rings onto a 9" (23cm) length of off-white grosgrain ribbon. Fold the cut edge of the ribbon under. Sew the folded-down end of the ribbon with off-white thread to secure the "D" rings.

three · Bring the needle up from the back of the ribbon and through the layered flower petals to stitch the wristband to the flower.

four · Thread the yellow crystal toggle button onto the thread so it rests in the flower center. Bring the needle back down through the layers of petal and ribbon, and repeat several times to secure the button. Knot the thread on the underside of the ribbon.

five · Fold over the other end of the ribbon, and sew it down to make a clean edge.

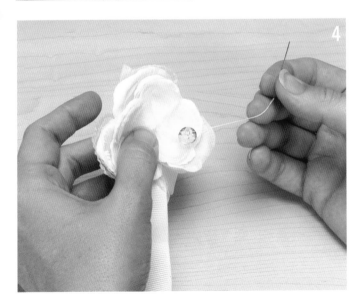

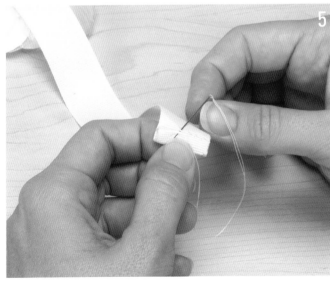

flowering shawl

tip > Consider presenting your bridesmaids with custom-made flower shawls that complement their dresses. Lengths of tulle are extremely affordable and are available in a wide array of colors, making this both an economical and easily customized project.

This delicate flowing wrap is the perfect accessory for an off-the-shoulder formal gown. The cascading rose-colored tulle is scattered with miniature pom-pom silk roses. Adding to the luxury of the finished shawl, each flower center features a small round pearl.

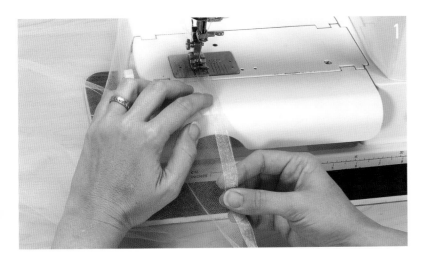

one · Fold the tulle in half lengthwise, and position the folded edge at the top of your work surface. Starting at the top right-hand corner, lay the ½" (1cm) wide pink organdy ribbon down over the right edge of the folded tulle. The ribbon should be half on the fabric and half off the fabric. Stitch the ribbon in place to fuse the ribbon and the two layers of tulle together.

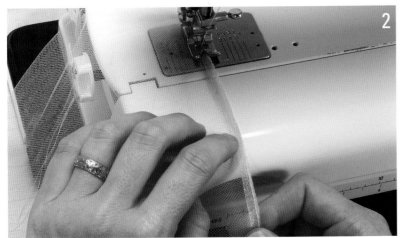

two · Fold the ribbon in half so the side of the ribbon that was not on the fabric now covers the underside. Make a second seam to stitch the folded ribbon in place. Repeat the process to edge the bottom and left open edges with ribbon.

three · Cut pom-pom rose silk flowers from their stems with wire cutters, and separate the petals (see Basic Techniques, page 13).

four · Begin sewing the flowers onto the shawl, attaching more roses at the left and right edges of the shawl and fewer toward the center. To sew on a flower, layer the petals together and hold them against the tulle. Bring the needle and thread up from the opposite side of the tulle and through the petals. Then string on a glass pearl to create the flower center.

five · Bring the needle back down through the petals and through the tulle. Turn the tulle over. Bring the needle through the layered petals of another flower and thread on a glass pearl. Bring the needle back down through the flower and up through the flower on the opposite side. Continue threading the needle up and down through both flowers until they are secure.

six · When you are satisfied that the flowers are sewn firmly in place, tie off the thread in between the flowers, next to the tulle.

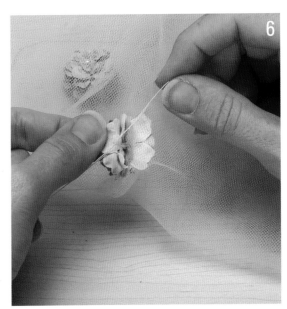

the beaded bride & company

Here comes the bride, all dressed in white, with attendants at her side…Once you select the dresses, it's time to think about accessories. Rather than pounding the pavement or searching online for the perfect piece of jewelry, consider making an original creation. You'll save yourself time and possibly discover a new passion for beadwork in the process.

This chapter is filled with necklaces, earrings, hair combs and even tiaras that are all a cinch to wire or string. Even the most novice beginner will have beading success. Once you get a feel for the process, you'll start looking at ready-made jewelry differently. Mass-produced pieces seldom use high-quality beads and clasps, but they're still quite costly.

Another benefit of making your own jewelry is how simply you can customize the designs. For instance, elongate or shorten a bride's necklace to flatter the neckline of her dress. You'll be amazed by the huge selection of beads on the market. Also consider adding charms or some of Grandma's old beads into your necklace to create original heirloom jewelry.

Making jewelry for your bridal party is a thoughtful and inexpensive way to express your appreciation for their part in your wedding. When making multiples, look for bulk packages of beads and clasps.

CHAPTER

4

glass flower tiara

MATERIALS

silver headband with combs (Darice)

26-gauge silver wire

6mm bicone crystal mix (Pure Allure)

4mm white glass pearls
(Cousin Corp. of America)

purple glass leaf beads

white flower beads

wire cutters

ANOTHER SIMPLY BEAUTIFUL IDEA

To make a smaller version of the tiara, simply twist the same bead sequences onto light-weight silver hair combs.

Crown your bridal ensemble with a beautiful handmade tiara. Select beads that accentuate your wedding gown—subtly-colored pearls and crystals are perfect choices. This tiara features three shades of violet punctuated with pearl-centered opaque lily flowers. You can easily hand-stitch a wedding veil behind the beads. Wire combs surround the headband, enabling it to stay in place through every hug on the receiving line.

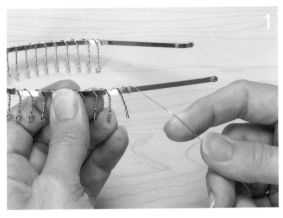

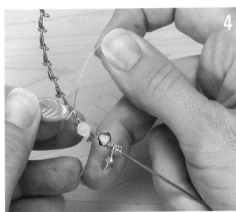

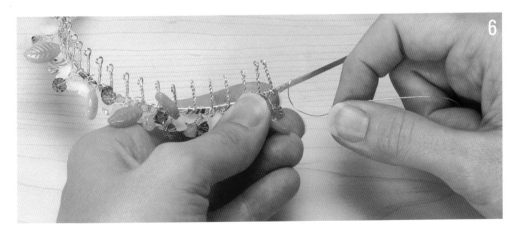

one · Wrap a long length of wire (approximately 3' [91cm] long), around one end of the headband to secure it.

two · Thread a crystal onto the wire so it rests ½" (1cm) from the headband, then fold the wire down.

three · Twist the wire to secure the bead.

four · Continue threading on beads and twisting the wire in the following pattern: Twist one each of the three different violet bicone crystals onto the headband, followed by a single leaf bead. Repeat the pattern until you reach the end of the headband. Secure the wire by wrapping it around the end of the headband.

five · Cut another 3' (91cm) length of wire, and secure it at the same spot where you secured the first wire. Slide on a flower bead, and bring it snug to the first row of beads. Slide a small pearl onto the wire so it nestles on top of the flower. Bring the wire back down through the flower center. Continue adding flowers around the headband, covering the front of the metal band and disguising the twisted wire holding up the first row of crystals.

six · Wrap the wire tightly around the end of the headband to secure it. To finish the headband, trim away any excess wire tail with wire cutters.

crystal bead hair combs

MATERIALS

1" (3cm) silver hair combs
(Hirshberg Schutz & Co.)

26-gauge silver wire

silver-lined glass leaf beads

clear glass leaf beads

clear glass disk-shaped beads

assorted clear, opaque and
silver-lined glass flower beads

clear "E" beads

wire cutters

The flowering glass beads on these combs bring a sparkle and shimmer to your hair that's perfect for an evening wedding. Beads are twisted onto different wire lengths that extend to capture the light. These combs are the perfect size to add a touch of evening glamour to your hairstyle without overpowering it.

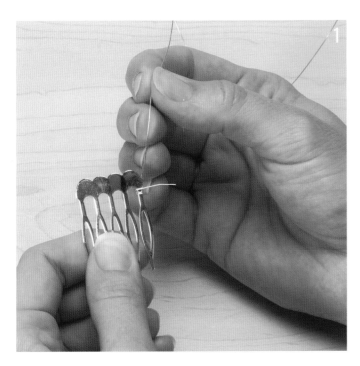

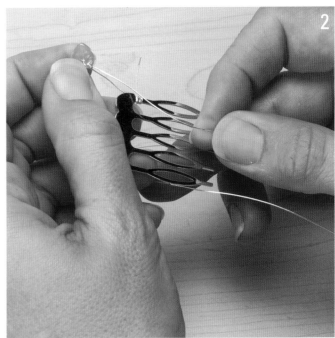

one · Cut about 2' (61cm) of wire and wrap one end around one of the teeth of the comb to secure it.

two · String on a clear leaf bead, and fold the wire back down toward the comb so there is about ½" (1cm) of wire between the top of the comb and the bead.

three · Twist the wire to secure the bead. There should be ½" (1cm) of twisted wire between the top of the comb and the bead. Wrap the wire around the comb before stringing on each new bead.

four · Continue stringing beads and twisting the wire in the following sequence: clear leaf on ½" (1cm) of twisted wire; silver-lined leaf on 1" (3cm) of twisted wire; and clear disk on ¼" (6mm) of twisted wire.

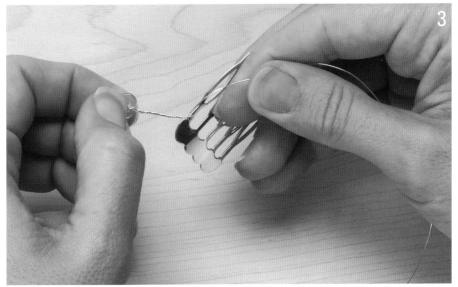

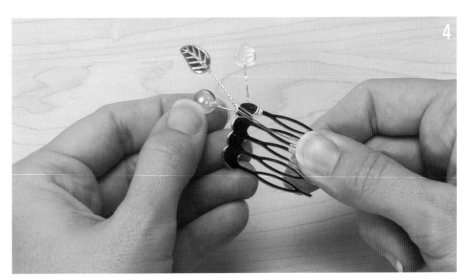

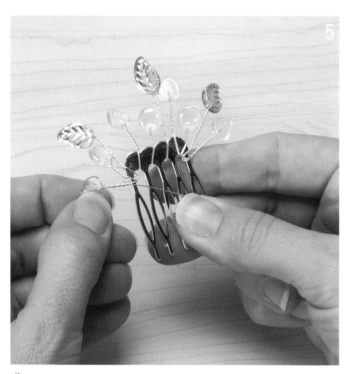

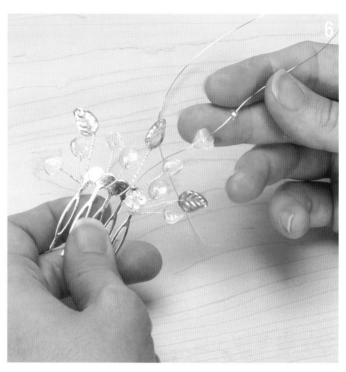

five · Continue beading until you reach the end of the comb. Wrap the wire around the last tooth in the comb to secure the first row of beads. Trim away any excess wire tail with wire cutters.

six · Cut another long length of wire, about 2' (61cm), and wrap the wire to secure it in the same place where you wrapped the first wire. String on a clear flower bead, and pull it snugly against the comb. Wrap the wire around the comb to secure this first bead.

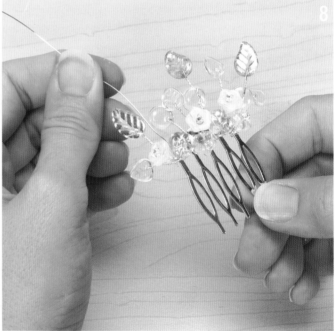

seven · Bring the wire back through to the front of the comb, and string on an opaque flower bead. Thread on a clear "E" bead and nestle it into the flower center. Bring the wire back down through the flower to secure the flower center. Wrap the wire around the comb to secure it.

eight · Continue beading the comb until you've completely concealed the front of the metal comb with flower beads. At the end of the comb, wrap the wire around the final tooth to secure the beading. Trim away any excess wire tail with wire cutters.

pink-knotted pearls

MATERIALS

pink natural silk cord with fixed needle no. 4 (Griffin)

6mm x 8mm cream oblong nugget pearls

leaf toggle clasp (Blue Moon Beads)

G-S Hypo Cement

straight pin or awl

scissors

B rightly colored silk cord provides a new twist on the traditional string of pearls. The result is that each individual pearl is framed with a pair of cheery pink knots. Both the genuine freshwater pearls and silk cord can be economically purchased in lengths at your local bead store. You'll be able to create elegant necklaces for all your bridesmaids without breaking your budget.

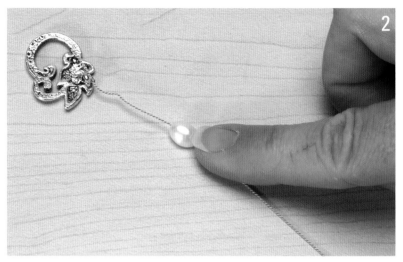

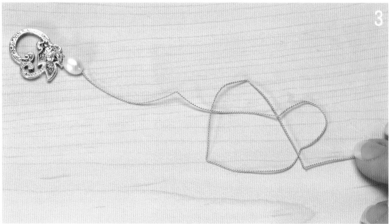

one · Cut a 2' (61cm) length of pink silk cord, and slide the clasp onto the end without the beading needle. Tie a knot in the cord to secure the clasp.

two · String the first pearl onto the cord, and slide it flush to the knot.

three · Tie a very loose knot in the silk cord a few inches from the first pearl.

four · Use a straight pin or an awl to push the knot back up the cord toward the pearl. When the knot is flush against the pearl, remove the needle or the awl from the middle of the knot and tighten it.

five · Continue beading and knotting until you've reached the finished beaded length, about 17" (43cm). Tie on the other end of the clasp.

six · Cut away any excess cord with scissors. Apply a dab of G-S Hypo Cement to strengthen the connection to the clasp at each end of the cording.

STAGGERED PEARLS

• THESE FLAT, ROUND PEARLS HAVE
been drilled off-center. To create this zigzag
pattern, simply alternate between stringing
them with the hole to the left and to the right.
I chose to complement the pattern with plain
white cord and an ornate vintage clasp.

one · Cut a 12" (30cm) length of white silk cord. Tie one end of a vintage pearl clasp to the end of the beading cord without the needle. String on 6mm round pearls until you reach a beaded length of 17" (43cm).

two · Tie on the remaining end of the clasp. Cut off the excess beading cord, and apply G-S Hypo Cement to the cord ends to secure the knots.

yellow flowers bracelet

MATERIALS

yellow teardrop (petal-shaped) beads

round, flat pearls

2" (5cm) sterling silver eye pins

lobster clasp with 1½" (4cm) chain

two 4mm silver jump rings

round-nose pliers

chain-nose pliers

wire cutters

tip > Switch to green petal beads to create four leaf clovers between each pearl. Regardless of whether your families are Irish or if one of your wedding colors is green, your bridal party will appreciate a little luck of the Irish at their fingertips.

Cleverly grouped yellow petal beads come together in this bracelet to make sunny glass flowers. Sterling silver eye pins link the flowers and freshwater pearls together to make an original and attractive bracelet.

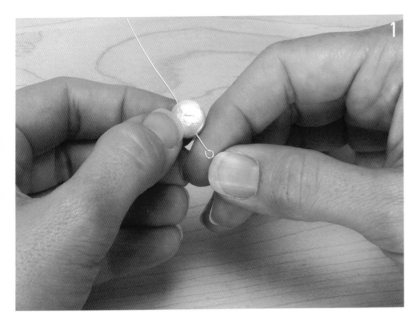

one · Thread a flat pearl onto a silver eye pin.

two · Bend the wire about ⅛" (3mm) above the bead at a 90° angle. Use round-nose pliers to make a loop. Make a wrapped loop by wrapping the wire tail around the base of the loop to secure it (see Basic Techniques, page 15).

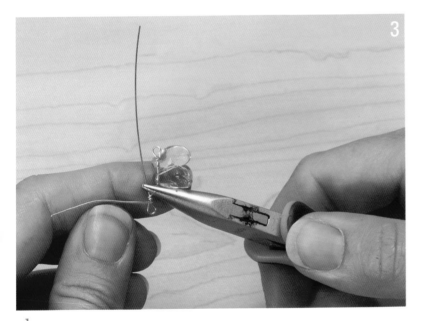

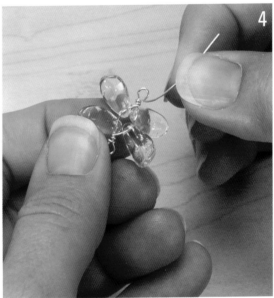

three · Begin to make the first yellow flower by threading two yellow petal beads onto an eye pin. With chain-nose pliers, wrap the straight end of the eye pin just above the base of the eye on a second eye pin.

four · Thread two more yellow petal beads onto the second eye pin, and wrap the straight end of the wire just above the base of the eye on the first eye pin.

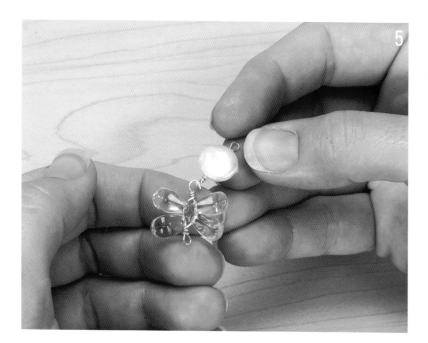

five · Open the loop on the flower eye pin, and attach it to the wrapped loop on the first flat pearl you made.

six · Continue to make flowers and pearls, and hook them together, alternating between the two. When you've completed the bracelet, you'll have four flowers and five pearls.

seven · Attach the lobster clasp to the first pearl in the bracelet with a 4mm silver jump ring.

eight · Attach a 1½" (4cm) length of chain to the eye pin loop of the last pearl in the bracelet.

nine · Slide a yellow petal bead onto an eye pin, and create a wrapped loop to make a dangle.

ten · Attach the yellow petal bead dangle to the end of the chain with a jump ring to finish the bracelet.

magnetic pearls

MATERIALS

34" (86cm) of .018" (.5mm) Beadalon stringing wire

6mm ivory magnetic beads (Magnetize by Westrim)

silver and gold mini bead mix (Blue Moon Beads)

no. 1 crimp bead (Beadalon)

chain-nose pliers

wire cutters

tip > When designing with magnetic beads, place them at regular intervals in the beading sequence to ensure the finished strand coils together and holds its shape.

Skip the clasps—this versatile length of beads uses magnetic power to coil together and stay connected. Until recently, most magnetic beads have resembled black hematite stones. Now they're available in different finishes, allowing you to create jewelry for formal occasions.

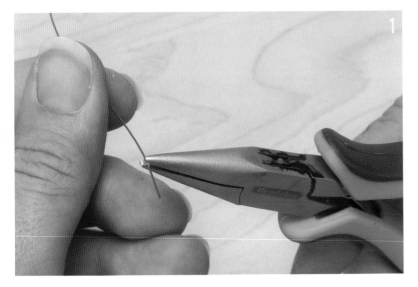

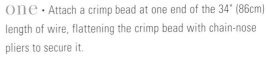

one · Attach a crimp bead at one end of the 34" (86cm) length of wire, flattening the crimp bead with chain-nose pliers to secure it.

two · Begin stringing beads in the following pattern: magnetic bead, silver rectangular bead, gold "E" bead, silver rectangular bead, gold rectangular bead, silver "E" bead, gold rectangular bead.

three · Continue stringing beads in the following pattern: magnetic bead, gold bead, silver "E" bead, gold bead, silver bead, gold "E" bead, silver bead.

four · Continue stringing beads in the established pattern, repeating steps 2 and 3 until you've reached a finished beaded length of about 30" (76cm). You should be able to coil the strand of beads four and a half times around your wrist.

five · Finish beading with a single magnetic pearl. Secure a crimp bead at the end of the beaded strand to finish the bracelet.

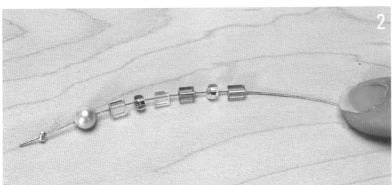

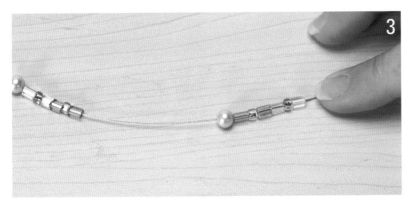

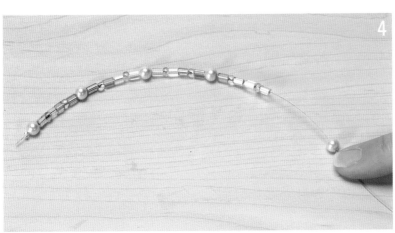

multistrand necklace

MATERIALS

eight 28" (71cm) strands of .015" (.4mm) Beadalon stringing wire

clear and pearl seed beads

AB bugle beads

AB and sandwashed "E" beads

4mm clear bicone beads

AB rectangle beads

8mm x 10mm crystal faceted glass beads

6mm opaque round beads

five-strand adjustable clasp (Blue Moon Beads)

crimp beads

clear tape

chain-nose pliers

BEAD SEQUENCES

Strand 1: 24" (61cm) in following sequence: alternate between AB bugles and pearl seed beads

Strand 2: 25½" (65cm) in following sequence: alternate between AB rectangles and pearl seed beads

Strand 3: 23½" (60cm) sandwashed "E" beads

Strand 4: 26¾" (68cm) in following sequence: pearl seed bead, clear seed bead, pearl seed bead, 4mm clear bicone bead

Strand 5: 23½" (60cm) in following sequence: pearl seed bead, sandwashed "E" bead, pearl seed bead, 8mm x 10mm crystal faceted glass bead

Strand 6: 22½" (57cm) clear seed beads

Strand 7: 23½" (60cm) in following sequence: five AB "E" beads, clear seed bead, AB rectangle, clear seed bead

Strand 8: 24" (61cm) in following sequence: five pearl seed beads, AB seed bead, opaque round bead, AB seed bead

Cascading lengths of crystal-clear, opaque, iridescent and sandwashed white beads are threaded in different sequences and joined together with a multistrand clasp to make this sophisticated necklace. The rich blend of glass beads creates a glamorous necklace that complements a simple satin bodice or enhances a plunging neckline. While you dance the night away, the free-flowing strands will swing with your every step.

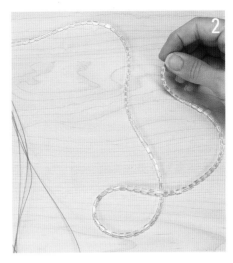

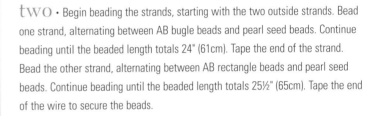

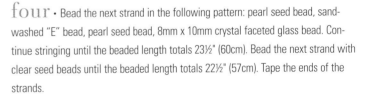

one · Attach a single 28" (71cm) strand of wire to each of the two end holes in a five-strand adjustable clasp with a crimp bead. For the center three holes, attach two wires to each hole using one crimp bead for each pair of wires.

two · Begin beading the strands, starting with the two outside strands. Bead one strand, alternating between AB bugle beads and pearl seed beads. Continue beading until the beaded length totals 24" (61cm). Tape the end of the strand. Bead the other strand, alternating between AB rectangle beads and pearl seed beads. Continue beading until the beaded length totals 25½" (65cm). Tape the end of the wire to secure the beads.

three · Bead one of the remaining inside strands with sandwashed "E" beads for 23½" (60cm). Bead the next strand in the following pattern: pearl seed bead, clear seed bead, pearl seed bead, 4mm clear bicone bead. Continue stringing until the beaded length totals 26¾" (68cm). Tape the ends of the strands.

four · Bead the next strand in the following pattern: pearl seed bead, sand-washed "E" bead, pearl seed bead, 8mm x 10mm crystal faceted glass bead. Continue stringing until the beaded length totals 23½" (60cm). Bead the next strand with clear seed beads until the beaded length totals 22½" (57cm). Tape the ends of the strands.

five · Bead the first strand in the final pair of wires in the following pattern: five AB "E" beads, clear seed bead, AB rectangle, clear seed bead. Continue string-ing until the beaded length totals 23½" (60cm). Bead the final strand in the following pattern: five pearl seed beads, AB seed bead, opaque round bead, AB seed bead. Continue stringing until the beaded length totals 24" (61cm). Tape the ends of the strands.

six · Remove the tape from each strand, one at a time. Attach the free ends of the wires to the other piece of the five-strand clasp. Attach the wires as for the first end of the clasp, attaching one strand to each of the outside holes and two strands to each of the three inside holes.

pearl cluster necklace

MATERIALS

16¾" (43cm) silver figaro chain
(Blue Moon Beads)

pink and pearl flat glass pearls
(Blue Moon Beads)

10mm and 8mm ecru glass
pearls (CCA Corp.)

2" (5cm) sterling head pins

1" (3cm) heavyweight head pins
(for flat pearls with larger holes)

6mm spring clasp

4mm jump ring

round-nose pliers

wire cutters

With its generous central cluster of glass pearls swinging from a filigree chain, this whimsical choker is a far cry from your grandmother's plain pearls. Your eye is drawn to the shimmering blend of pearl shapes in varying sizes and colors. At the back of the choker, a single flat disk pearl adds interest to the adjustable clasp, and multiple disks add to the volume in the center of the cluster.

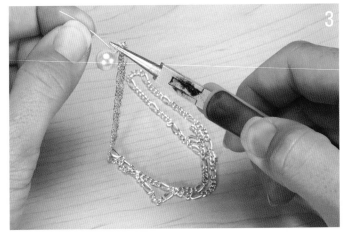

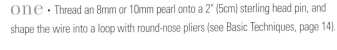

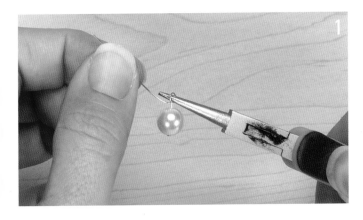

one • Thread an 8mm or 10mm pearl onto a 2" (5cm) sterling head pin, and shape the wire into a loop with round-nose pliers (see Basic Techniques, page 14).

two • The pearl dangles in this necklace will all be clustered along the center 5" (13cm) of the necklace. To find the starting point, fold the length of chain in half to find the center. Measure out 2½" (6cm) from the center, and slide the head pin with the pearl from step 1 onto a link in the chain at that point. This dangle marks one border of the 5" (13cm) of dangles.

three • Wrap the tail of the wire around the base of the loop to secure the pearl dangle (see Basic Techniques, page 15). Trim away the excess wire tail with wire cutters.

four • Slide a pink flat glass pearl onto a heavyweight head pin, and cut the head pin wire about ⅜" (1cm) above the bead. Turn a loop in the top of the head pin wire to create a loop. Hook the dangle to the chain, and close the loop to secure it to the link.

five • Continue to attach the round pearls with wrapped sterling head pins and the flat pearls with looped heavyweight head pins onto the individual chain links. Concentrate the smaller pearls toward the sides of the arrangement. After linking each dangle to the chain, clip any excess wire tail with wire cutters.

six • Use a jump ring to attach the clasp to one end of the chain. Slide a final large flat pearl onto a heavyweight head pin, and attach it to the other end of the chain to make a dangle.

glass teardrop necklace

MATERIALS

five 20½" (52cm) strands of .015" (.4mm) Beadalon stringing wire

4mm x 9mm crystal glass daggers (Halcraft)

AB seed beads (Blue Moon Beads)

fold-over crimp ends

two 4mm jump rings

2" (5cm) chain

hook clasp

tape

chain-nose pliers

round-nose pliers

wire cutters

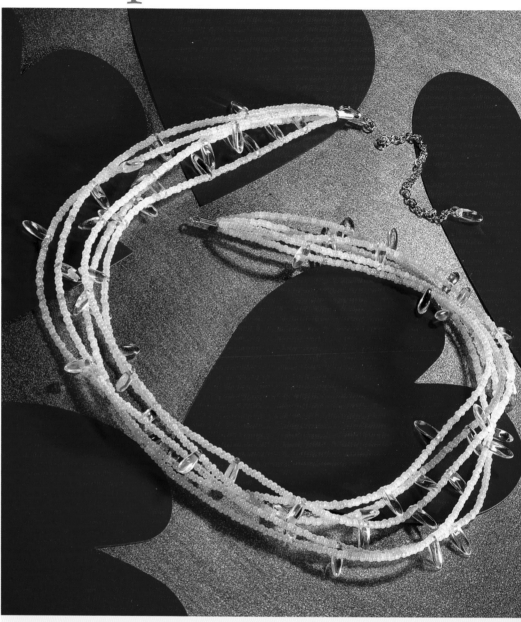

This beautiful collar of beads is comprised of five strands of tiny seed beads punctuated with teardrop-shaped beads. The iridescent sheen comes from the aurora borealis coating applied during the manufacturing of the beads. The individual beaded lengths are joined at the ends with fold-over crimps and an adjustable-length chain clasp.

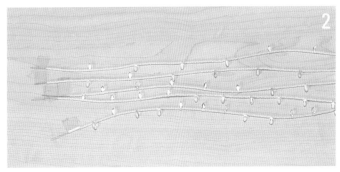

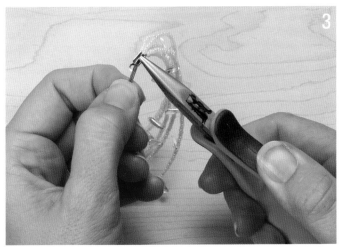

one · Tape the end of one 20½" (52cm) strand of stringing wire. Thread on ¾" (2cm) of AB seed beads, and then thread on a glass dagger. Continue stringing on seed beads punctuated by glass daggers at ¾" (2cm) intervals until the beaded length totals 18" (46cm). Tape the free end of the wire.

two · Bead the remaining strands with seed beads and glass daggers. For each strand, the daggers will be spaced a little differently to create a staggered effect. The length of each strand will also differ. Strand two: 1" (3cm) interval, 18¼" (46cm) length; Strand three: ¼" (6mm) interval, 18" (46cm) length; Strand four: 1¾" (4cm) interval, 19" (48cm) length; Strand five: 2" (5cm) interval, 19" (48cm) length. Tape the end of each strand.

three · Remove the tape from one end of the strands. Bundle the ends together and feed them down the center of one of the fold-over crimp ends. Use round-nose pliers to fold each flap over to secure the bundled strands. Repeat for the other end of the strands. Trim the wire ends.

four · Use a 4mm jump ring and chain-nose pliers to attach one piece of the hook clasp to the hole in the fold-over crimp end at each end of the necklace.

five · Open the last chain link to attach the length of chain to the other fold-over crimp end. Open a jump ring and slide on a crystal dagger. Slide the jump ring onto the last link in the chain, and close the jump ring.

crystal and pearl bracelet

MATERIALS

two 9" (23cm) strands of .015" (.4mm)
Beadalon stringing wire

6mm white glass pearls
(CCA)

6mm rhinestone crystal rondel spacers

rhinestone-studded metal heart pendant
(Blue Moon Beads)

sterling silver rope toggle clasp
(CCA)

no. 2 crimp tube with a twist
(Beadalon)

tape

chain-nose pliers

wire cutters

This simple pearl and rhinestone bracelet is versatile enough to complement any formal gown, and it makes an ideal gift for attendants in your bridal party. The bracelet features a sparkling heart-shaped charm that dangles by the toggle clasp. Small rhinestone-studded disks integrate the sparkle of the charm into the double strands of pearls.

one · Tape one end of a 9" (23cm) length of wire. String on three pearls, a rhinestone rondel spacer and six more pearls. Continue stringing on a rhinestone spacer and six pearls three more times and end with three pearls.

two · Tape one end of another 9" (23cm) strand of wire. String on six pearls and a rhinestone spacer. Repeat this pattern a total of five times. End with six pearls.

three · Remove the tape from both wires at one end. Slide a pendant onto both wires.

four · Thread a crimp tube onto the wires, and then thread the wires through the hole in the "O" end of the toggle clasp. Thread the wires back through the crimp tube, and flatten the crimp tube with chain-nose pliers.

five · Attach the bar end of the toggle clasp to the other end of the bracelet with a crimp tube. Trim away any excess wire tail with wire cutters.

rhinestone flowers necklace

MATERIALS

four 22" (56cm) strands of .015" (.4mm)
Beadalon stringing wire

nine rhinestone flower spacers
(Crystal Innovations, Pure Allure)

silver-lined seed beads

two fold-over crimp ends

4mm jump rings

jewel toggle clasp
(Pure Allure)

tape

chain-nose pliers

wire cutters

Graduated lengths of tiny seed beads are strung between rhinestone flowers to form a series of connected scallops in this eye-catching choker. The beaded lacework creates a uniquely shaped choker that gracefully contours your neckline. Both the sparkling silver-lined seed beads and rhinestones make this piece the perfect complement to a low-cut formal gown.

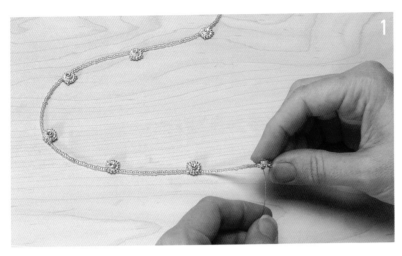

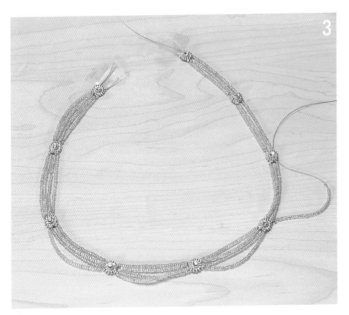

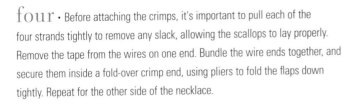

one · Tape one end of a 22" (56cm) strand of wire. String on a rhinestone flower spacer followed by 32 seed beads. Continue stringing beads in the same pattern a total of eight times. Finish the strand with a final rhinestone flower spacer. Tape the free end to secure the beads.

two · Tape the end of a second 22" (56cm) strand of beading wire. Thread it through the same hole in the flower spacer as the first wire, and then thread on 34 seed beads. Continue in this pattern until you have strung the second wire through all the rhinestone flower spacers. Tape the free end of the wire.

three · For the third strand, tape the end of a 22" (56cm) strand of wire, and thread it through the second hole in the first rhinestone flower spacer. String on 36 seed beads, and repeat as for the first two strands. String the final strand through the second hole as well, stringing on 38 seed beads between each spacer.

four · Before attaching the crimps, it's important to pull each of the four strands tightly to remove any slack, allowing the scallops to lay properly. Remove the tape from the wires on one end. Bundle the wire ends together, and secure them inside a fold-over crimp end, using pliers to fold the flaps down tightly. Repeat for the other side of the necklace.

five · Use jump rings to attach one end of the clasp to each end of the necklace to finish.

vintage glass flower earrings

MATERIALS

clip-on earrings
(Westrim)

4mm ecru glass pearls
(CCA)

blue glass roses
(Blue Moon Beads)

26-gauge silver wire

round-nose pliers

wire cutters

Like a pair of earrings you might discover tucked away in Grandma's jewelry box, both the color and size of these earrings are reminiscent of the 1940s. The center of each earring features a delicate glass flower framed by a circle of ecru glass pearls.

one · Use round-nose pliers to twist the end of a 6" to 8" (15cm to 20cm) length of wire into a small loop.

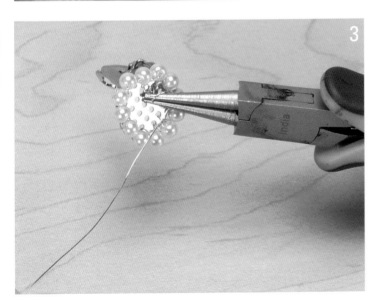

two · Thread the wire through a hole at the edge of the clip-on earring base so the loop stays on the top. Thread a pearl onto the wire.

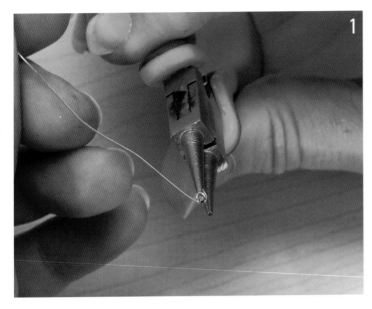

three · Thread the wire down through the next hole, keeping the pearl on the top. Continue threading the wire through the holes around the outside edge and stringing on pearls until the earring is completely encircled in a ring of pearls. Finish where you began by trimming the wire end and shaping it into a loop to secure.

four · Push the green stem of a glass rose through the center hole of the earring from front to back.

five · Working on the underside of the earring, cut the green stem with wire cutters and push the very tip of the wire back up through an adjoining hole to secure the flower. Use pliers to pull the stem back through and to bend the end slightly to secure it. Repeat to make the second earring.

Wire small pearls to the outside of the clip-on earring to create a ring of pearls. Then insert the green stems of the pink flowers through some of the center holes of the clip-on earrings and secure the ends as for the other earrings. Repeat to make the second earring.

PINK GLASS FLOWER EARRINGS

• INSTEAD OF JUST ONE GLASS FLOWER, THIS VARIATION USES a smaller flower and leaves. Carefully arrange all three glass pieces so they fit within the pearl ring. Pull the stems all the way through the earring back to check the fit. Make any necessary adjustments before trimming and shaping the wires.

delicate gold earrings

MATERIALS

clear rhinestone rings
(Beadin' Path)

white pearls with flat backs

gold lever back earrings

gold jump rings

26-gauge gold wire

chain-nose pliers

wire cutters

They say diamonds are a girl's best friend, and in this case they may not be the real thing, but the dazzling effect is the same. Each of these earrings features a ring of sparkling rhinestones that adds drama to the lustrous single-pearl centers.

one · Thread a small piece of gold wire through the center of a pearl.

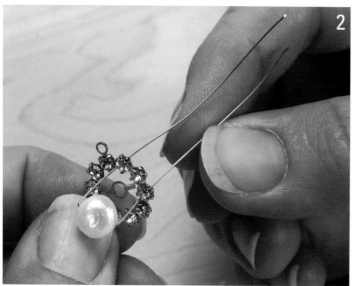

two · Bend the gold wire into a "U" shape, and pull the wire ends through a clear rhinestone ring.

three · Twist the ends of the gold wire together to secure the pearl.

four · Trim the ends with wire cutters, and use chain-nose pliers to bend the twisted wire down.

five · Open a jump ring, slide it onto the lever back earring, and slide on the rhinestone ring with the pearl center. Close the jump ring to finish (see Basic Techniques, page 15). Repeat to make the second earring.

To make these earrings, simply slide a purple teardrop pearl onto a gold head pin and cut the wire about ³/₈" (1cm) above the bead. Use round-nose pliers to turn a loop in the head pin wire (see Basic Techniques, page 14), and slide the loop onto the bottom loop of a purple rhinestone diamond. Close the loop securely with pliers. Attach a lever back earring wire to the top loop to finish. Repeat to make the second earring.

PURPLE PEARL EARRINGS

• THIS EARRING VARIATION IS DISTINGUISHED BY THE SUBTLE

shade of lilac that shines in both the rhinestones and in the drop-style pearl.

chandelier princess earrings

MATERIALS

freshwater rice pearls
(Blue Moon Beads)

chandelier earring forms
(Pure Allure)

sterling silver ball earwires
(CCA)

sterling silver ball head pins
(CCA)

round-nose pliers

wire cutters

ANOTHER SIMPLY BEAUTIFUL IDEA

No matter what chandelier finding and beads you select, transforming them into earrings always follows the same steps. This pair of hearts features sparkling crystals hanging from shaped head pins. They're the perfect accessory for a Valentine wedding.

You'll feel like royalty when you slip on these ornate earrings. Despite their elaborate appearance, they're deceptively easy to assemble. Choose from a wide selection of premade rhinestone-studded findings, and then simply hang pearls or crystals from the bottom loops.

one · Slide a freshwater pearl onto a head pin, and cut the wire ³⁄₈" (1cm) above the bead.

two · Shape the head pin by turning a loop in the end of the wire with round-nose pliers (see Basic Techniques, page 14).

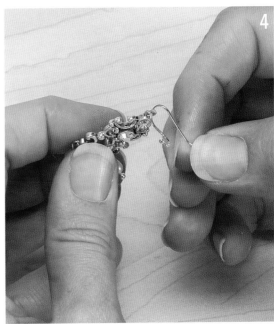

three · Create two more pearl dangles, and attach all three to the earring form.

four · Thread the earwire through the top hole in the finished chandelier.

felt jewelry pouch

MATERIALS

6½" x 10¾" (17cm x 27cm) piece of
sturdy felt with decorative edging

10¾" (27cm) length of ⅞" (2cm)
wide cream satin ribbon

two snap buttons

thread

sewing needle

straight pins

straightedge

fabric scissors

sewing machine

This little pouch is the perfect way to present and store handmade jewelry gifts. Its slender shape and soft surface are ideal for any of the bracelets or necklaces featured in this chapter. Scalloped felt quickly folds into an envelope—all you need to keep it together is to machine-stitch the side seams and hand-sew a couple of snaps to the front flap.

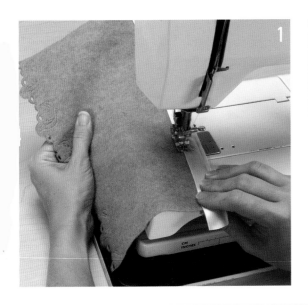

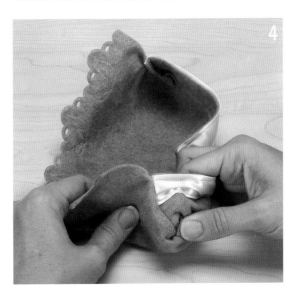

one · Sew a 10¾" (27cm) length of ⅞" (2cm) wide cream ribbon along the straight, long edge of the 6½" x 10¾" (17cm x 27cm) felt piece, making two seams. Sew the ribbon on the right side of the felt.

two · Fold the felt lengthwise up 2¼" (6cm) from the ribbon edge. Pin the felt into a pouch shape.

three · Use the sewing machine to sew the seams up the sides. To make the finished pouch less bulky, trim the edges close to the seam, and cut across each bottom corner diagonally.

four · Turn the pouch right-side out, making sure to poke the corners out completely.

five · Sew on two snaps on either side of the ribbon and on the flap.

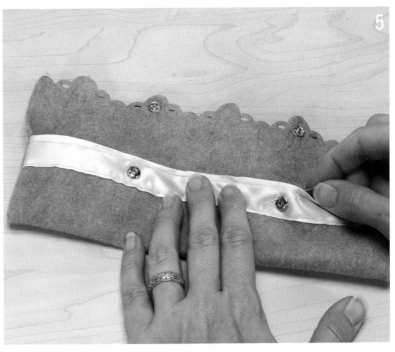

resources

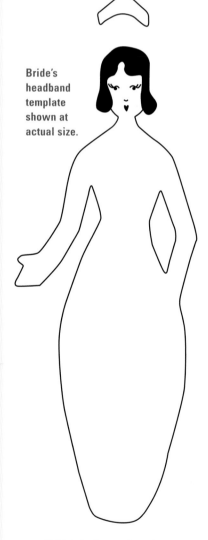

Bride's headband template shown at actual size.

Bride's body template shown at actual size.

Enlarge bride's dress template at 133% to bring it to full size.

ANNA GRIFFIN

888.817.8170

www.annagriffin.com

scrapbook papers, stamps, ribbon

BEADALON

www.beadalon.com

stringing wires, findings, beads, tools

BEADIN' PATH

877.922.3237

www.beadinpath.com

vintage rhinestone findings, Japanese seed beads

BLACK INK (GRAPHIC PRODUCTS CORPORATION)

www.gpcpapers.com

decorative leaves

BLUE MOON BEADS

800.377.6715

www.bluemoonbeads.com

beads, jewelry findings, heart charms

CCA CORP.

800.366.2687

www.cousin.com

glass pearls

COLORBÖK

800.366.4660

www.colorbok.com

scrapbook papers

C.R. GIBSON

800.243.6004

www.crgibson.com

photo album, guest book

DARICE

866.432.7423

www.darice.com

silk flowers, heart-shaped rice, metal combs and headbands, jewelry findings, beads

DUNCAN

800.423.6226

www.duncancrafts.com

Aleene's Glues

EVERLASTING ELEGANCE

floral arranging solution

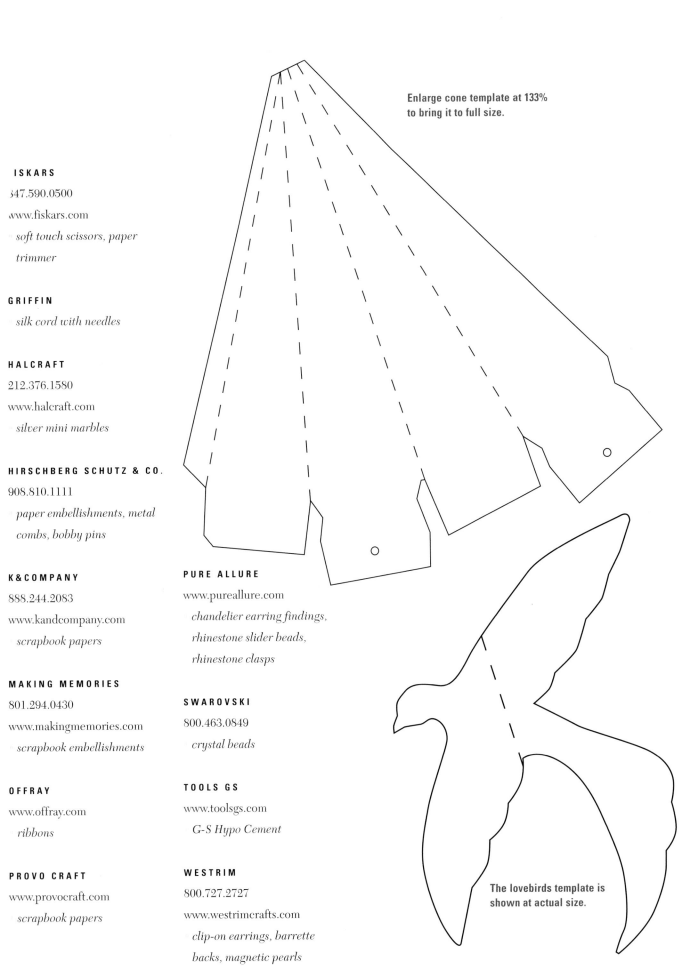

Enlarge cone template at 133% to bring it to full size.

ISKARS
847.590.0500
www.fiskars.com
soft touch scissors, paper trimmer

GRIFFIN
silk cord with needles

HALCRAFT
212.376.1580
www.halcraft.com
silver mini marbles

HIRSCHBERG SCHUTZ & CO.
908.810.1111
paper embellishments, metal combs, bobby pins

K&COMPANY
888.244.2083
www.kandcompany.com
scrapbook papers

MAKING MEMORIES
801.294.0430
www.makingmemories.com
scrapbook embellishments

OFFRAY
www.offray.com
ribbons

PROVO CRAFT
www.provocraft.com
scrapbook papers

PURE ALLURE
www.pureallure.com
chandelier earring findings, rhinestone slider beads, rhinestone clasps

SWAROVSKI
800.463.0849
crystal beads

TOOLS GS
www.toolsgs.com
G-S Hypo Cement

WESTRIM
800.727.2727
www.westrimcrafts.com
clip-on earrings, barrette backs, magnetic pearls

The lovebirds template is shown at actual size.

index

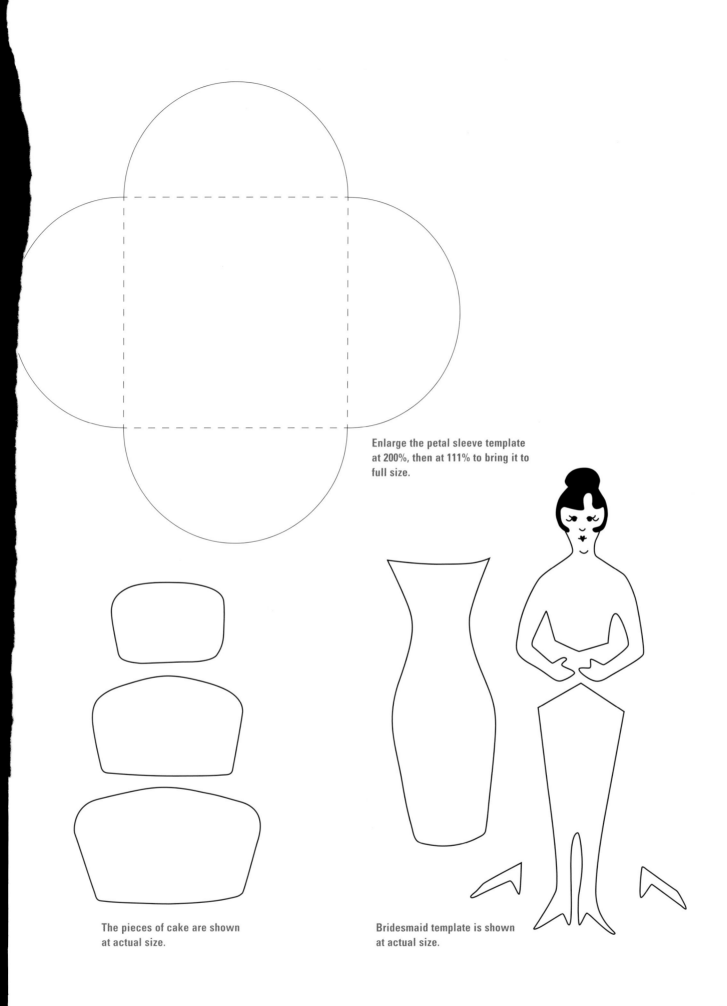

Enlarge the petal sleeve template at 200%, then at 111% to bring it to full size.

The pieces of cake are shown at actual size.

Bridesmaid template is shown at actual size.

TRY THESE OTHER GREAT TITLES FROM NORTH LIGHT CRAFT

● **THESE BOOKS AND OTHER FINE NORTH LIGHT TITLES** are available from your local arts-and-crafts retailer, bookstore or online supplier.

SIMPLY BEAUTIFUL BEADED JEWELRY
BY HEIDI BOYD

This book is filled to the brim with over 50 gorgeous beaded necklaces, bracelets, earrings and accessories. Author and designer Heidi Boyd's trademark style shines in each of the projects and variations. Best of all, every piece is simple to make and beautiful to wear. Even a beginning crafter can easily finish any project in one afternoon. The book includes a helpful techniques section and insightful tips scattered throughout.
ISBN-10: 1-58180-774-0, ISBN-13: 978-1-58180-774-5, paperback, 128 pages, 33445

WEDDING PAPERCRAFTS
FROM THE EDITORS OF NORTH LIGHT BOOKS

In projects using the latest techniques in papercrafting, rubber stamping and collage, *Wedding Papercrafts* shows you how to create your own invitations, decorations and favors. All of the projects show you how to personalize your wedding with unique handmade touches. The book includes 50 gorgeous projects made easy with patterns and step-by-step instruction. ISBN-10: 1-55870-653-4, ISBN-13: 978-1-55870-653-8, paperback, 128 pages, 70603

NEW INSPIRATIONS IN WEDDING FLORALS
BY TERRY L. RYE

With the simple and clear instruction in this book, you'll learn to create beautiful wedding florals that look professionally crafted. Whether you're an experienced flower arranger or a beginner, this book provides expert tips and techniques to make your wedding even more lovely. Included are 30 unique, step-by-step projects with variations such as bridal and bridesmaid bouquets, arrangements for the ceremony, table centerpieces, cake toppers and more! ISBN-10: 1-55870-634-8, ISBN-13: 978-1-55870-634-7, paperback, 128 pages, 70582

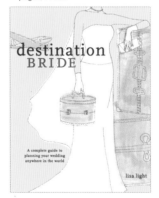

DESTINATION BRIDE
BY LISA LIGHT

Destination Bride is the go-to guide for any couple planning to marry away from home. International wedding consultant Lisa Light provides information on how to plan every aspect of a destination wedding, from choosing the location and setting a budget to making travel arrangements and coordinating the ceremony. The book also provides overviews on specific locales around the world, including maps and color photos. There's even a section covering the nitty-gritty details of a destination wedding, with information on marriage laws and currency exchange.
ISBN-10: 1-55870-703-4, ISBN-13: 978-1-55870-703-0, paperback, 383 pages, 70654